Love
Aunty Marie 2012

Beatrice Marie Anderson

Nlakapmux Grandmothers' Stories

How generations of Indigenous Grandmothers of British Columbia carried out their responsibilities to transmit knowledge

LAP LAMBERT Academic Publishing

Impressum/Imprint (nur für Deutschland/only for Germany)
Bibliografische Information der Deutschen Nationalbibliothek: Die Deutsche Nationalbibliothek verzeichnet diese Publikation in der Deutschen Nationalbibliografie; detaillierte bibliografische Daten sind im Internet über http://dnb.d-nb.de abrufbar.
Alle in diesem Buch genannten Marken und Produktnamen unterliegen warenzeichen-, marken- oder patentrechtlichem Schutz bzw. sind Warenzeichen oder eingetragene Warenzeichen der jeweiligen Inhaber. Die Wiedergabe von Marken, Produktnamen, Gebrauchsnamen, Handelsnamen, Warenbezeichnungen u.s.w. in diesem Werk berechtigt auch ohne besondere Kennzeichnung nicht zu der Annahme, dass solche Namen im Sinne der Warenzeichen- und Markenschutzgesetzgebung als frei zu betrachten wären und daher von jedermann benutzt werden dürften.

Coverbild: www.ingimage.com

Verlag: LAP LAMBERT Academic Publishing GmbH & Co. KG
Heinrich-Böcking-Str. 6-8, 66121 Saarbrücken, Deutschland
Telefon +49 681 3720-310, Telefax +49 681 3720-3109
Email: info@lap-publishing.com

Approved by: Vancouver, The University of British Columbia, Diss., 2011

Herstellung in Deutschland (siehe letzte Seite)
ISBN: 978-3-8484-0098-0

Imprint (only for USA, GB)
Bibliographic information published by the Deutsche Nationalbibliothek: The Deutsche Nationalbibliothek lists this publication in the Deutsche Nationalbibliografie; detailed bibliographic data are available in the Internet at http://dnb.d-nb.de.
Any brand names and product names mentioned in this book are subject to trademark, brand or patent protection and are trademarks or registered trademarks of their respective holders. The use of brand names, product names, common names, trade names, product descriptions etc. even without a particular marking in this works is in no way to be construed to mean that such names may be regarded as unrestricted in respect of trademark and brand protection legislation and could thus be used by anyone.

Cover image: www.ingimage.com

Publisher: LAP LAMBERT Academic Publishing GmbH & Co. KG
Heinrich-Böcking-Str. 6-8, 66121 Saarbrücken, Germany
Phone +49 681 3720-310, Fax +49 681 3720-3109
Email: info@lap-publishing.com

Printed in the U.S.A.
Printed in the U.K. by (see last page)
ISBN: 978-3-8484-0098-0

Nlakapmux Grandmothers' Traditional Teachings and Learnings

by

Beatrice Marie Anderson

B.I.S.W., The Nicola Valley Institute Technology

and The University of Regina, 1992

M.S.W., The University British Columbia, 1993

A THESIS SUBMITTED IN PARTIAL FULFILLMENT OF

THE REQUIREMENTS FOR THE DEGREE OF

DOCTOR OF EDUCATION

in

THE FACULTY OF GRADUATE STUDIES

(Educational Leadership and Policy)

THE UNIVERSITY OF BRITISH COLUMBIA

(Vancouver)

December 2011

Abstract

Nchwa' squest. My name is Beatrice *Tiila* Marie Anderson. I am *Nlakapmux*, a social worker, educator, mother, wife, Grandmother, and great Grandmother. Not all learning in Indigenous communities is attained through formal institutional settings. Much of our important learning comes from Indigenous Knowledge (IK) passed on through family and social contexts. This research examines, documents, and contributes to knowledge about how generations of Indigenous *Nlakapmux* Grandmothers from the Interior of British Columbia carried out their responsibilities to transmit *Nlakapmux* educational and socio-cultural knowledge to their family and community members. Grandmothers are a critical part of the family's social learning environment. This knowledge is important to understand because traditional family pedagogies were and continue to be at the heart of how *Nlakapmux* children learn and how *Nlakapmux* knowledge and values are transmitted and sustained. The process of colonization lessened this important approach to Indigenous intergenerational learning.

A *Nlakapmux Grandmother's Methodology* was developed that includes a *Spilahem* story of my life history; an analysis of historical and contemporary literature about the *Nlakapmux* people; and interviews and circle talks with 11 *Nlakapmux* Grandmothers. The *Nlakapmuxcin* Indigenous language, wholistic Plains Medicine Wheel, and metaphor of the *Nlakapmux* cedar root basket making were used to analyze and make meaning of the Grandmothers' stories.

The findings highlight eight *Nlakapmux* principles for teaching and learning that form the basis of a *Nlakapmux Developing Wisdom Theory*. They include: (1) *Takemshooknooqua,* Knowing we are connected: land, animals, plants and people; (2) *ChaaChawoowh,* Celebrating people and land joyously; (3) *Huckpestes,* Developing lifelong learning and wisdom; (4) Huztowaahh, Giving lovingly to family and community; (5) *Choownensh,* Succeeding in endeavours; (6) *Choowaachoots,* Utilizing Nlakapmux vision-seeking methods; (7) *Nmeenlth coynchoots,* Incorporating Nlakapmux knowledge; and (8) *Peteenushem,* Reflecting on learning and relearning lifelong lessons.

These findings and the *Nlakapmux Developing Wisdom Theory* have implications for current and future child rearing practices, and family and community educational practices. This form of intergenerational family focused Indigenous knowledge is vital to the *Nlakapmux* people and needs to be consciously revitalized, transformed into current day pedagogy and practice, and transmitted to younger *Nlakapmux* generations.

Preface

This work is approved by:

The University of British Columbia Behavioural Research Ethics Board

Certificate number H09-01968

Cook's Ferry Indian Band - on date September 1, 2009

Table of Contents

Abstract ... iii

Preface ... iv

Table of Contents ... v

List of Tables ... viii

List of Figures ... ix

Nlakapmux Language Glossary ... x

Acknowledgements ... xii

Dedication ... xiii

Chapter One: Introduction ... 1
- **1.2 Research Purpose** ... 3
- **1.3 Research Questions** ... 3
- **1.4 Locating Nlakapmux People through Land, Language, and Stories** 4
- **1.5 A Colonial Story of *Nlakapmux* People** ... 7
- **1.6 *Shinkyap*/Coyote and *Nlakapmux* Stories** ... 13
  - 1.6.1 *Speta'kl* Stories ... 14
  - 1.6.2 *Spilahem* Stories ... 17
- **1.7 Language Issues** ... 19
- **1.8 Theoretical Framework: Double-Voice and Double-Consciousness 24**
- **1.9 Thesis Chapter Descriptions** ... 28

Chapter Two: Methodology ... 31
- **2.1 Introduction to Indigenous Research** ... 31
- **2.2 An *Nlkapmux* Grandmother's Methodology** ... 34
- **2.3 Storywork** ... 38
  - 2.3.1 Respect ... 40
  - 2.3.2 Responsibility ... 40
  - 2.3.3 Reverence ... 41
  - 2.3.4 Reciprocity ... 41
- **2.4 Participant Selection** ... 41
- **2.5 Analysis** ... 48
- **2.6 Summary** ... 50

Chapter Three: *NCHAWA SPILAHEM*: My Story ... 53
- **3.1 My Origin** ... 60

3.2 Early Memories of Travel and Schooling 67
3.3 Conscientization, Coming of Age, and Leadership 71
3.4 Formal Education, Indigenous Studies, and Eldership 79
3.5 Case Study 4: Marie Anderson 81
3.5.1 Physical Realm 82
3.5.2 Mental Realm 83
3.5.3 Spiritual Realm 85
3.5.4 Emotional Realm 87
3.4.5 Volitional Realm 88
3.6 Discussion and Summary 89

Chapter Four: Outsider and Insider Stories about the Nlakapmux 99
4.1 *Tshama Toohoosh*: In The Eyes of The Other 99
4.2 *Speta'kl*: In Our Songs 105
4.3 *Shinkyap Nlakapmux*: Tracks in our Nlakapmux Landscape 110
4.4 Discussion and Summary 116

Chapter Five: *NLAKAPMUX* Grandmother Voices 125
5.1 Introduction 125
5.2 Introducing the Grandmother Participants 126
5.2.1 May Voght (Moses) 127
5.2.2 Patsy McKay (Philips) 127
5.2.3 Jean York (Albert), Laxpetko 127
5.2.4 Leona Lafferty 128
5.3 *Nlakapmux* Sibling Biographies 129
5.3.1 Lorna Sterling (Anderson), *Chinmalx* 129
5.3.2 Trudine Dunstan (Anderson) 130
5.3.3 Judy Blades (Anderson), *Lamiinak* 130
5.3.4 Aiona Carmelita (Anderson) 131
5.3.5 Bernice Anderson, *Whatpalx* 131
5.3.6 Verna Billy-Minnabarriet 132
5.3.7 Yvonne Shuter, *Shepeenak* 133
5.4 Medicine Wheel: Wholistic Analysis 134
5.5 Cedar Root Basket Making: *Nlakapmux* Grandmothers' Knowledge 144
5.5.1 Physical Realm 147
5.5.2 Spiritual Realm 151
5.5.3 Emotional Realm 156
5.5.4 Mental Realm 160
5.6 Summary of *Nlakapmux* Grandmother Perspectives 165

Chapter Six: *Caustem* (Using) *Nlakapmux* Teachings and Learnings 170

6.1 ***Nlakapmux*: Developing Wisdom Theory** **171**
6.2 ***Takemshooknooqua*: Knowing We are Connected - Land, Animals, Plants,**
and People **174**
6.3 ***ChaaChawoowh*: Celebrating People and Land Joyously** **177**
6.4 ***Huckpestes*: Developing Life-long Learning and Wisdom** **181**
6.5 ***Huztowaahh*: Giving Lovingly to Family and Community** **186**
6.6 ***Choonwensh*: Succeeding in Endeavours** **190**
6.6.1 "The Poor Hunter Story" as told by *Shinkyap*/Coyote 193
6.7 ***Choowaachoots*: Utilizing *Nlakapmux* Vision-Seeking Methods** ... **194**
6.8 ***Nmeenlth Coynchoots*: Incorporating *Nlakapmux* Knowledge** **202**
6.9 ***Peteenuushem*: Reflecting on Learning and Relearning Lifelong Lessons** **207**
6.10 Summary **212**
Chapter Seven: *Waasheet*: Beginning a New Journey **217**
7.1 ***Nlakapmux*: Developing Wisdom Theory (NDWT)** **217**
7.2 **Implications for Application of the Research** **220**
7.3 **Significance and Contribution of the Research** **222**
7.4 **Implications for Future Research** **225**
7.5 **Personal Reflections from a Nlakapmux Grandmother and Scholar 227**
7.6 **Conclusion** **233**
References **241**
Appendix A: Questions for the Nlakapmux Grandmothers **247**

List of Tables

Table 1. ***Nlakapmux*** **Grandmothers' Wholistic Chart 82**
Table 2. **My** ***Spilahem*** **Beaver Teachings 142**

List of Figures

Figure 1.	**Family and Map of *Nlakapmux* Territory**	**4**
Figure 2.	**Semxelc'e Family and Territory**	**33**
Figure 3.	**Three Grandmothers: Tilaa, Lamiinak, and Alice**	**37**
Figure 4.	***Nlakapmux* Chiefs with James Teit**	**64**
Figure 5.	**Original of Light**	**71**
Figure 6.	**Anderson Family: August 2001**	**77**
Figure 7.	***Nlakapmux* Perspectives' Wheel**	**101**
Figure 8.	***Nlakapmux* Developing Wisdom Theory**	**105**
Figure 9.	***Nlakapmux* Intergenerational Learning**	**112**

Nlakapmux Language Glossary

Ahuckpestena – I learned

Atch'ha'ma – Vision Quest

Ayee – I am awake

Caustem – Using

ChaaChawoowh – To be joyful

Choownensh – To succeed

Choowaachoots – To develop

Coynchoots – Our knowledge and ways

Hanla – How are you?

Huckpestes – To have learned, developing wisdom

*Huztowaahh – T*o love one another

K'K'ze – Grannys

klip klip – Dark

Kookshchamuh – Thank you "you saved my life"

Kulthkulthmeen – Old Ones, old people, Elders

Nchwa' squest – My name is

Nlakapmux – Thompson People, the Thompson Tribe

Nlekepmxcin – Thompson Speakers

Nmeemlph – We the people

Peteenushem – Reflective thinking, thought

Peymanoos – Place name means "large bare place"

Piluhachin – I tell you

*Pokais*t – Place name means "little white stones"

Quanata – Look at, see the

S-choo – Work

Sepeetza – Name meaning “blanched”

Shau’a’tem – Ask them

Shinkyap – Coyote

Sheestkin – Pit house

Shooshum, Soopalalie – Soapberry

Shwatken – Who am I?

Skaloola – Owl

Spetakl – Old stories

Spilahem – Current stories

Spopza – Grandpa

Sumehalza, Shuumahalza, Semelc a – Great-grandfather’s name meaning, “living spirit”

Takemshooknooqua – all my relatives

Tmix – Earth, dirt land, territory

Toohoosh – Eyes

Tsamoolaawhh – Bigfoot

Tseeuush – The way it is

Tshama – White person (Other)

Washeet – Walk

Yameet – Pray

YaYa – Great-granny

Acknowledgements

I would like to thank: Drs. Jo-ann Archibald, Q'um Q'um Xiiem, Graham Hingangaroa Smith and Francis Lee Brown for their insight, support and guidance. I also want to convey my thanks to Professors, Dr. Gregory Cajete, Dr. Sandy Grande, Dr. Lester Irabinna Rigney, Dr. Linda Tuhiwai Smith and Dr. Bob Morgan for sharing their Indigenous theories, enthusiasm and undying interest in the summer classes of 2007.

I wish to express my gratitude to *Nlakapmux* Grandmother interviewees and collaborators, both living and in the spirit world, for their willingness to share their family experiences and their Indigenous Knowledge.

A special thank you to my family, without whom this would not have been possible, to my cohort, advisor Dr. Jo-ann Archibald, and my committee, Dr. Rosalyn Ing and Dr. Jean Barman.

Finally, many thanks to my colleagues for their support and help as listeners and editors and for their limitless love and support!

My appreciation to James Teit, for the photos of my family that are featured in the archival document, held by the Museum of Civilizations in Gatineau, Québec.

Dedication

To my great grandchildren and our ancestors the *Nlakapmux* family of *Semxelce* (Timothy) and the *Whatpalx* (Clara Edmonds) lineage not documented.

To my sister Virginia Grace Mirehouse (Anderson) (1947-2002).

To the *Nlakapmux* people, ancestors, born and unborn.

To all Indigenous people the world over, who have a dream and vision for Seven Generations hence!

For the Great Spirit, the great mystery our Creator.

Chapter One: Introduction

Nchwa' squest. My name is *Teelahah* Beatrice Marie Anderson. I am a great-grandmother, grandmother, mother, educator, and social worker. In this thesis, I share *Nlakapmux* (Thompson, Interior Salish) pedagogical lessons that I have learned through close intergenerational experiences with Grandmothers of my Indigenous community located in the Interior of British Columbia.

Not all learning in First Nations[1] communities is attained through formal institutional settings. Much of our important learning comes from Indigenous knowledge passed on through family and social contexts. More specifically Grandmothers[2] as Elders are a critical part of the family's social learning environment. This knowledge is important to document because traditional family pedagogies were at the heart of how *Nlakapmux* children learned and how *Nlakapmux* knowledge and values were transmitted and sustained.

---

[1] First Nations, Aboriginal, and Indigenous are used interchangeably throughout the thesis. First Nations refers to people who are registered with an Indian Band, but I prefer to include those who are members of a First Nation through kinship. Aboriginal includes First Nations, Metis, and Inuit as per the definitions in the Canadian Constitution. The term Indigenous includes local and international reference to First Peoples of various lands. I use these and other terms such as "Indian" to reflect their usage in various time periods and the usage of authors whom I discuss and cite.

[2] Throughout the thesis, the first letter of Grandmother is capitalized as a symbol of respect for Grandmothers who teach others.

These lessons have implications for current and future child rearing practices, and family and community educational practices. This form of family focused Indigenous knowledge is vital to the *Nlakapmux* people and must not be lost. It needs to be overtly identified, consciously encouraged, revitalized and developed amongst our younger *Nlakapmux* generations. Another urgent reason for this research is that many *Nlakapmux* people who are fluent language speakers and cultural knowledge holders have died or have completely lost their language fluency through the destructive colonial influences of the Indian Residential Schools, and laws that banned cultural ceremonies making it incumbent upon but not limited to remaining fluent speakers and cultural knowledge holders, like myself, a Grandmother, to pass it on to others. Grandmothers have had and some continue to carry out this important role of teaching and mentoring to their grandchildren.

In this chapter I introduce my research purpose and questions; provide an historical and contemporary context of *Nlakapmux* people and their communities, introduce two genres of *Nlakapmux* stories that are used througout the thesis, discuss the issue about language usage, highlight aspects of my theoretical framework, and conclude with a description of the thesis chapters.

1.2 Research Purpose

The goal of this research is to examine, describe, document and contribute to knowledge about how Indigenous *Nlakapmux* Grandmothers carried out their responsibilities to convey informal and formal *Nlakapmux* educational and socio-cultural knowledge to their family and community members through intergenerational interaction.

Grandmothers' ways of passing down their knowledge occurred during family meals, family activities and community gatherings. The Grandmothers historically and presently use storytelling pedagogy to pass on their knowledge. These stories are called *Spilahem*. The term "pedagogy" shows the inextricable link between lifelong teachings and how the learner becomes teacher and vice versa. I illustrate points from the selected use of my mother tongue, the *Nlkapmuxcin* language, to describe meanings not evident in the English language and to emphasize the unique teachings or learnings that are conveyed.

1.3 Research Questions

From the perspectives of *Nlakapmux* Grandmothers:

1. How did Grandmothers pass on *Nlakapmux* knowledge (values, beliefs, and teachings) and pedagogy?
2. What were important teachings and pedagogies?
3. How did *Nlakapmux* intergenerational learning, oral tradition, and teachings contribute to living a good life?
4. Which *Nlakapmux* teachings and pedagogies are practiced in the Grandmothers' families today?
5. What are the challenges and opportunities for continuing these Nlakapmux teachings and pedagogies in family and community settings?

The next section presents both historical and contemporary information about *Nlakapmux* people and our communities in order to provide a historical, geographical, social, political, and educational context in which to understand this study and its research questions.

1.4 Locating Nlakapmux People through Land, Language, and Stories

I remember my Grandmother, *Lameenak*, telling me that we were called the *Nlakapmux* because "*Nmeelph a shyatkimwhaaw weeahh na koouii* (we are the people who are living along the pure river)." The explanation for our former official (colonizer) name, space and place is that we the *Nlakapmux* were 'discovered' by the explorer David Thompson, so that we became known as Thompson Indians. We are officially further divided and categorized into two main groups: Lower Thompson, extending along the Fraser River canyon from just south of Lytton to an area just South of Spuzzum, and Upper Thompson, consisting of four subgroups in an area extending from Lytton up the Fraser River to about 20 kilometers below Lillooet (See Figure 1). This includes the Thompson River drainage system from its mouth upriver to Ashcroft and the Nicola River drainage, including a large area around Merritt (approximately 25 kilometers radius from Merritt). However, we now refer to ourselves by our original name, *In-thla-CAP'mu-wh*, or *Nlakapmux*. I use the spelling, *Nlakapmux*, throughout my thesis.

In this historical categorisation, my people are today defined as *Interior Salish* and divided into four nations: *Shuswap* (now *Secwepemc*), *Thompson* (now *Nlakapmux*), *Okanagan and Cheetwhawt* (my spelling). Although *Okanagan* territory extends into Washington State, in Canadian maps the *Okanagan Tribe* ends at the 49th parallel. Our tribal neighbours include the *St'at'imcets* (their spelling) or *Lillooet* communities that are divided into two main groups linguistically, culturally and geographically: the Upper or Fraser river Lil'wat/*Lillooet*, mainly in the vicinity of the current town of *Lillooet* on the Fraser River, *and* the community of Mount Currie in the Pemberton Valley that extends south to *Skookumchuk.* We all speak dialects of the *Salishan* language. The following map, Figure 1, shows the original boundaries of our boundaries.

Figure 1. Map of *Nlakapmux* Territory

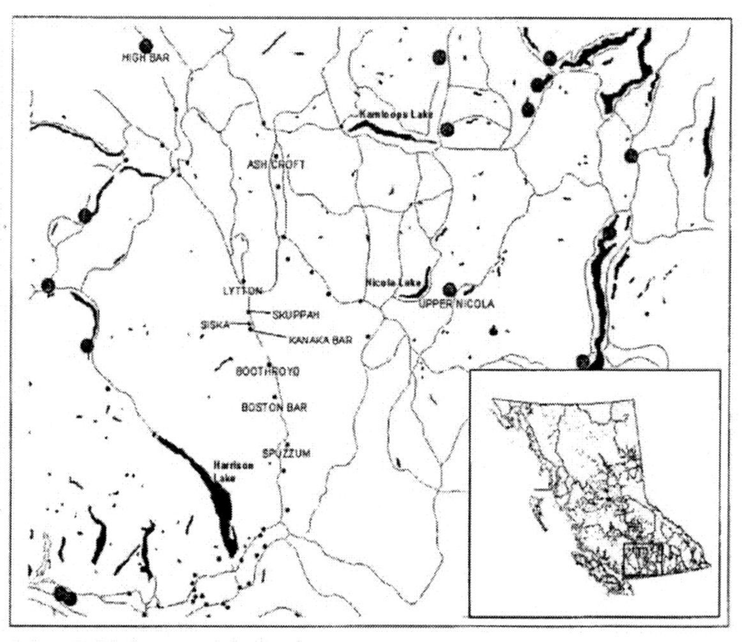

Map of Nlaka'pamux original territory -

For my family and myself, pre-European contact means to have lived in pre-English language times or exclusively in the *Nlakapmuxcin* language, traditions and experiences of our ancestors. In my own family, and before me, "old people" passed on to us what it was to be *Nlakapmux* in those times through narratives and stories, which each of us has incorporated into our very being. These times, at the turn of the century, were rich in legends and traditional songs, sung with no need to interpret the *Nlakapmuxcin* words. From a study of these songs emerge teachings for correct behaviour. First Nations people of my Tribe have lived and survived along the Thompson river for centuries prior to the arrival of Anglo-explorers, Simon Fraser in 1808 and David Thompson a little later. We were (then) known to our neighbours, as the "people of the river." "We traded with our neighbours of the four directions to fulfill our daily needs." (Grandmother Tiilaa story told to Marie Anderson,1950).

1.5 A Colonial Story of *Nlakapmux* People

Our history of European contact and colonization holds many negative experiences and traumatic memories which are still preventing our full participation in mainstream society. This period is defined as "dark times" for us. In this section, I mention key events such as the loss of territory, the imposition of the *Indian Act,* the Residential School era, and subsequent cultural identity losses to illuminate the drastic changes that occured with European contact. This colonial history has, since contact, circumscribed our Indigenous place and space in our own territory and culture, therefore, it is a reflection of our history through the lens of the "other."

Living along the banks of the Fraser river in south western British Columbia, the *Nlakapmux* people had a long history of contact with non-Aboriginal peoples. The *Nlakapmux* were in the path of the Cariboo road, the Canadian Pacific Railway (CPR) and virtually every other commercial and province-building initiative undertaken in the region (Laforet & York,1998, p. 85).

The gold rush began in 1858, in which thousands of people traveled through *Nlakapmux* territory, to arrive in the Northern goldfields. Of course, the Canadian Pacific Railroad had its inception not long thereafter and was completed by 1885. By this time the *Indian* Act had been established and the Indian Reserves legally surveyed and allotted. The *Nlakapmux* people did not surrender their territory nor treaty for their traditional lands.

A second railroad, The Canadian Northern Railway, now known as the Canadian National Railroad (CNR), was built and completed by 1915, making two railroads, crossing *Nlakapmux* territory on both sides of the Thompson river. The gravel rip rap used by the railroads to support the train tracks destroyed the natural eddys of the currents which salmon used to navigate to their spawning river.

Nlakapmux struggles for land ownership had its origins in the period 1850 – 1875. A document prepared by James Teit in 1928, on behalf of the *Nlakapmux,* was presented to Queen Victoria about the ownership of *Nlakapmux* territories. *Nlakapmux* political and community leaders have steadfastly defended these land claim issues to present day.

Politically, British Columbia became two colonies by 1863: the Vancouver Island colonial governor was appointed in 1851 and the Mainland colonial governor was appointed in 1858. The population of the new Mainland colony was approximately 26,000 Aboriginals and 6,514non-Aboriginals (Barman, 2007, pp. 421-430). In 1876 the *Indian Act* defined who was an Indian and the *Department of Indian* Affairs was created. Among the destructive policies subsequently enacted included the policy that an Indian woman marrying a non-Indian or Indian man who did not have Indian status resulted in the loss of her Indian status.

From the inception of the *Indian Act* in Canada, many new constructs were conceived for the Indigenous population in Canada. This included definitions of who is an "*Indian*" and dictating where they would live, how they were to be educated and governed. From first contact, *Nlakapmux* people began to see the Indigenous names changed of their personal family, community, group, nation, and territory, down to everything that constituted our natural and material world. Other traumatic changes occurred under colonial power. The traditional family and community units were impacted significantly by the Residential School era. *Nlakapmux* children attended Residential schools in Lytton and Kamloops, British Columbia. Most attended St. George's Residential School in Lytton. A sketch of this school's historical origins, enrollment, and health issues are presented next.

The early beginnings of educational schooling in British Columbia began in 1867 by the Anglican Church of Canada, whose goal was to evangilize, administer to the sick and to provide basic schooling to the Aboriginal population. In *Nlakapmux* territory, Reverend John Booth Good of the Anglican Church moved his mission from Yale to Lytton, opening an Indian Boys' School in 1902. Financial hardship caused a lease of land and agreement with the Federal Government in 1922, after which the original school became *St.*

George's Residental School. The Federal Government financed the school and the Anglican clergy took charge of school administration and hiring teachers. The girls who had previously attended *All Hallows School* at Yale were moved to *St. George's Residential School* in Lytton in 1917. The schooling for boys and girls went to grade eight. The new school was under quarantine for most of 1926-27 due to health issues affecting 95 students and resulting in 13 deaths. In 1927, Ottawa builds a new school with a capacity for 180 children. The old school was demolished in 1929. The Indian children suffered a measles' health crisis in 1936-37. The school continued educating children to grade 9 from 1930-49.

By 1952, the Residential school was deemed overcrowed with 212 Indian children in residence. Indian children from areas outside the *Nlakapmux* also attended this school. In the 1950's changes occurred where the children still lived at the Residential school but some started to attend the public school. For example, 50 Indian students attended high school in nearby Lytton, B.C. In 1962 all children who lived at the Residential school attended public school in Lytton. In 1967 the *St. George's Residential* S*chool* is renamed *St. George's Student Residence*. During the 1970's the enrollment drops drastically as children from the Nass Valley, Hazelton and Kitaamaat are phased back into their communities. By 1976, only *local* Nlakapmux children were enrolled. The school was closed in July 31, 1979 (http://www.anglican.ca/relationships/trc/histories/st-georges-school-lytton/).

The colonial story continues today with Indigenous people in Canada struggling to revitalize Indigenous languages and cultures, to settle outstanding land claims, to realize self-determination, and to improve all aspects of our lives (Royal Commission on Aboriginal Peoples, 1996). The *Nlakapmux* Nation today has two Tribal Councils and several independent Indian Bands with an estimated population of 6,000 people. The exact total numbers are not known because of the diversity of *Nlakapmux* governance. To provide an example of this diversity, the two Tribal Councils are described. The *Nlakapmux Nation Tribal Council* today has seven member Indian Bands and a registered population of 3100 people, with approximately 56% of this population living off reserve (http://www.gov.bc.ca/arr/firstnation/nlakapamux_nation/default.html). The Nicola Valley Tribal Association lists eight Indian Bands as members with a registered population of 2618 people and approximately 56% of this population live off reserve (http://dsp-psd.pw.gsc.gc.ca august 30,2011).

Despite the historic presentation of oppression presented above and the diversity of *Nlakapmux* governance today, it is my belief that Indigenous *Nlakapmux* values, philosophy and beliefs still prevail. This colonial story is a useful context to my own story that speaks about the colonial impact on our life as *Nlakapmux* people. Being an *Nlakapmux* woman living in this society today, I feel outrage, hurt and pain about our colonial history and its impacts. I wonder how can this be? When will we be heard? Who will help us? I feel I am capable and worthy to be considered a human being with human rights, however, I think that is not true or possible for future generations unless drastic transformation occurs to regain and revitalize our Indigenous languages, cultures, families, and communities. *Shinkyap*, where are you?

1.6 *Shinkyap*/Coyote and *Nlakapmux* Stories

My Great-Grandmother, *Lamiinak*, shared the story, *Lakashstique,* about the origin of light with me, when I was a little girl (see story in Chapter Four). She also told me many other origin stories that included the magic of trickster and transformer, *Shinkyap*, Coyote. My use of the concept of Coyote is therefore most appropriate in developing the transformational theme of my thesis. In our oral tradition *Shinkyap*/Coyote is the vehicle of transmission with threads linking the teachings from generation to generation.

I have followed *Shinkyap*/Coyote tracks in our *Nlakapmux* natural landscape, as well as reading and gleaning knowledge from texts written by Indigenous and non-Indigenous scholars. *Shinkyap*/Coyote took on the role of teacher and assisted me with theoretical understandings that helped me make meaning of the various stories that I heard and experienced while on my thesis research journey. *Shinkyap*/Coyote has the reputation of making magic and being a trickster in order to make his lessons enjoyable and of interest. Therefore, Coyote stories and the metaphor or function of *Skinkyap* could be considered a form of pedagogy that affirms our place in the world, a point thoroughly missed by early outsiders' written works.

I have also followed *Skinkyap* tracks in the stories of a sample of *Nlakapmux* Grandmothers who are part of my extended family network and community with whom I have conducted interviews. In order to better understand the nature of *Nlakapmux* stories, I describe two genres that are used throughout my thesis: *Speta'kl* and *Spilahem.*

1.6.1 *Speta'kl* Stories

Our knowledge of our history begins in Myth time, the period of time that Western scholars call pre-historical times. These stories of how creation occurred and how we became human beings were passed orally from generation to generation in creation and transformational stories and songs. These stories describe our world before the white man came. Our world contained descriptions and stories about our history, kinship lines, prophecy of existence, our connection to each other and the cosmos.

Our people's textbook was Mother Nature's palette. Our people were scientists as they communicated with the universe. We were spiritual beings and embodied the entire universe. We were alive within the bosom of Earth Mother. Following European contact our oral *Speta'kl* were translated and became written stories when early travelers, traders, ethnographers and anthropologists came to our territory and began to document our legends.

These legends not only describe our natural world - the skies, the mountains, the rivers, the trees, the plants, the animals – but also our intimate relationship and connectedness with that world and our knowledge of it. In these ancient stories, transformer beings taught us how to live with all creation and gave us instructions to live a balanced, good life as human beings, families and communities. Our people believed "[a]nimals and supernatural beings moved through a land well populated and replete with historical references. The stars and constellations overhead commemorated the journey of the Transformer to our territories" (Laforet & York, 1999, p.209).

The *Nlakapmux* stories and songs, including the *Shinkyap* (Coyote) stories, relate explicitly to the origins of the Tribe and how the Creator sent Coyote to transform objects and geography for tribal use, including instructions for the use of all creation in *Nlakapmux* territory. Indeed, in the case of oral *Nlakapmux* history the *Shinkyap* is the link between the past and today. We are still surrounded by our history today. The transformer stories that guided *Nlakapmux* living in myth times are still valid today – they tell us who we are and give us an idea of the physical and spiritual world in which we live. These legends tell us about the vast and wealthy natural territory we inhabited and our complex, rich spirit and psyche.

Our *Speta'kl* stories are complex and have many different functions, and a fundamental belief we hold is related to the concept of transformation that is noted in the quote below.

> In myth times, humans and animals were said to have the same faculties. Not only were they capable of communicating with each other, but they were also able to exchange physical forms. Typical transformations include changing from being dead to being alive, being sick to being healthy, being poor to being rich, being animal to being human, being human to being animal, being animal to being things (Laforet & York, 1999, p.41).

The process of transformation in our stories offers profound meanings and the process of passing on of these stories illumine the capacity and power that is given to us to transform.

Shinkyap/Coyote, the transformer, was present at the beginning of our contact with Europeans, which is the time where the light originally given to *Nlakapmux* in *Lakashstique,* the origin of light story, began to become hidden and the dark began to come back. I describe the subsequent return of light, not through the accounts of others (colonizers), but through *Nlakapmux* reclaiming *Spilahem* (current narrative) and research.

1.6.2 *Spilahem* Stories

This thesis story situates me in a place and space that is congruent with my people's way of passing on their knowledge through stories, both *Speta'kl* (creation stories) and *Spilahem* (personal telling) which has always been the way of my people, particularly my family. We have maintained our original connection to our world and to ourselves as *Nlakapmux* families and communities, despite the changing times. Our worldview of creation is fully alive with ourselves comprising a part of this universe of energy. The transformers gave us profound and long held knowledge of the infinite web that connects us with this universe.

We started to tell *Spilahem* stories when the dark came back (the start of colonization) although it seemed like a long absence and silence before our voices and stories were heard. We are fortunate that our Grandmothers still held onto the *Speta'kl* stories and passed them on to us as secret flames of knowledge to keep for a future time that would see the transformers return and bring back the light to our world. The light has begun to come again to our world and we can tell *Spilahem* stories about our resistance to colonization and how we have maintained our Indigenous Knowledge. We also tell these *Spilahem* stories so that others can learn about the devastating impact of colonization and most importantly appreciate our resilience and persistence to keep our Indigenous languages, stories, and values alive.

This journey of the return of the light is a symbol of the continuity of our *Nlakapmux* history and culture. This belief in continuity is crucial in healing the social dislocation we were subjected to since the arrival of Europeans. As an *Nlakapmux* person, a Grandmother, a *Kulthmeen*, a scholar and educator, I reaffirm the belief that our oral traditions are the most lasting and effective methods of *Nlakapmux* education because they have survived. They have an application in contemporary educational pedagogy and praxis. I use the term 'praxis' to indicate cultural practice based on traditional customs that are transformed for current usage. One key challenge is to portray the *Nlakapmuxcin* concept into English written words.

1.7 Language Issues

My ability to share what I know is challenging because this thesis is predominantly written in a foreign language: English. To counter this form of hegemony, I chose to honour my identity as an *Nlakapmux* person and the *Nlakapmuxcin* language by first using *Nlakapmuxcin* concepts to convey meanings and understandings that I gained through my research. The *Nlakapmuxcin* concepts are then translated into English (see Glossary). A pressing concern is that our *Nlakapmuxcin* language loses meaning when translated to English.

I use a phonetic form of *Nlakapmuxcin* that uses my own spelling because there is not one consistent way to portray our *Nlakapmuxcin* in written form at the present time. In fact there are two written forms being used: the Randy Bouchard version used by Hannah and Henry (1995) in their book, *Our*

Tellings: Interior Salish Stories of the Nlakapmux People. The other is the Thompson River Salish Dictionary (Thompson & Thompson, 1996). I chose to spell my written version phonetically because the other two written versions were developed by non-*Nlakapmux*. The phonetic version is how *Nlakapmuxcin* sounds when it is orally told. I share a short *Spilahem* story to illustrate the differences in language functions and the difficulty when one language function and structure is imposed upon another.

In elementary school when we were asked to recount "what happened during your holiday," I wrote about the scene of a car accident and I remember quoting in my story, the words uttered by the accident victim: "I feel like hell." The teacher said that my story was unacceptable as it contained the word "hell." Although I pointed out that it was in quotation marks, the teacher said to me: "We do not use those words here." I had been telling my story, using my own language references, in the style of old, where recounting experiences as they literally happen is acceptable. I learned that language is judged as was the case here. The word "hell" was not acceptable for a girl of my age to use. As shown in my example, I learned quickly that the English moralistic style did not match my *Nlakapmuxcin* satiric language. Indeed, the two languages' expressions of similar stories were substantially different. This is the reason why today I reflect quite purposefully and look up definitions to ensure I am representing my *Nlakapmuxcin* point of view accurately in English. This problem of reconciling two different language forms and meanings is also discussed in another section in this chapter "on double-voice" and demonstrated in Chapter Four.

The problem with misunderstanding the meanings in our oral literature is not only due to the difficulty in translation; perhaps of greater concern is the unfamiliarity of "others" to understand and appreciate it. In fact, Indigenous oral tradition is often regarded as being merely descriptive and lacking any depth of meaning (Ross, 1996). Our oral stories have often been dismissed as inferior and primitive, and misunderstood by Western societies, not only because they were unwritten, but because in their eyes our stories did not conform to the conventions of Western literary criticism and literary standards. This is why my examination of ethnographic works such as those of James Teit (1900) and Franz Boas (1940) caused me to wonder about the accuracy of some of the documented information, not only because of the language and cultural differences between the parties, but the hegemonic sentiment of the day, which is a greater concern. The question begging to be asked was: "When written by an outsider, how valid is the Indigenous knowledge when it is portrayed through the lens or bias of the writer/recorder?" I return to this question when I review the *Nlakapmux* literature in Chapter Four. Our language is a rich web of meanings connecting us with the vast spiritual, psychological, mental and physical dimensions of life in this world and in the entire universe of creation. My point about the richness and complexity of our languages and the difficulty in interpreting and translating them into English, is also supported by Indigenous scholars such as Cohen (2010), Vedan (2002), and Archibald (2005, 2008).

Indigenous people, along with their cultures and languages, were viewed and researched as if they were artifacts to be collected and identified, rather than understood as cultural equals. Because of this Western way of viewing Native societies and their traditions as primitive, it is understandable that artistic elements characteristic of oral traditions went unnoticed by early Western researchers. More recently, this view is changing with efforts by researchers who appreciate and create relevant and ethical scholarship about Indigenous ontology and epistemologies. Linda T. Smith (1999) affirms this point in her book, *Decolonizing Methodologies: Research and Indigenous Peoples*. A mainstream scholar, Jan P. Van Eijk (2010), who studies Indigenous languages, acknowledges the meticulous categories of concepts inherent in Indigenous languages attesting to centuries of observation, collection, and analysis. She stresses the need to acknowledge the epistemological value of Indigenous languages and to appreciate the diversity of languages, instead of emphasizing just the use of English.

> First Nations languages are bottomless and boundless. Every word you record is a jewel and if it's lost because the last surviving Elder who knows these words dies, that's it. It's a great loss to humanity. There is so much wisdom in each word or phrase....Every language encodes knowledge in its own unique way. We cannot base the general psychology, how people think, how they classify language, how they classify reality, on just one language (i.e. English) (Van Eijk, 2010, p.1).

My personal experience as a speaker of my mother tongue and my knowledge of Grandmother Stories, *Speta'kl* (past stories) and *Spilahem (current stories)*, reinforces the epistemological quality and complexity of both *Nlakapmuxcin* and our stories. Most of these elemental characteristics were ignored and went unnoticed by early ethnographers and anthropologists when they collected and preserved our *Speta'kl* in written record from oral storytellers. They meticulously collected and recorded stories, documenting them in English; therefore, they are often incomplete or inaccurate.

The complex stylistic features that were characteristic of oral Speta'kl (traditional) stories were not understood or appreciated (Hanna & Henry, 1996). Though misunderstood by the early ethnographers, these early records are the closest representations of oral *Speta'kl* stories of the day at the time of colonial contact. They allow us some access to the surviving oral tradition of the pre-contact period (Stigter, 2003, p.42).

Since colonial contact and the ensuing acts of assimilation and acculturation Indigenous languages and the oral traditions communicated through these languages were legislated into silence by the Federal Government for a period of at least 125 years. Since the powers of the Federal Government and the 'Churches' denied Indigenous people in Canada their right to practice their cultures and languages for such a long time period, we need to acknowledge Indigenous people's tenacity and perseverance to maintain their cultures and languages in view of these impositions. In my search for literature about *Nlakapmux* people in pre to early contact, I felt that I needed a theoretical understanding of how to address the scholarship that was written by outsiders about us. I needed some way to reconcile the Western framework that was used to portray our Indigenous oral tradition. I found the concepts of "double-voice" and "double-consciousness" particularly helpful (Stigter, 2008). These terms made me wonder if *Shinkyap* had spent time with Stigter.

1.8 Theoretical Framework: Double-Voice and Double-Consciousness

In her work *Double-voice and Double-consciousness in Native American Literature*, Shelley Stigter (2008) makes a clear case for this phenomenon of double-voice and double-consciousness that is apparent in her collection of translated Native stories, which describe Native culture and life. When I encountered these terms, I felt they described me looking at me from another's perspective.

Stigter (2008) draws on Bakhtin's and Zolbrod's concept of double-voice. She uses Bakhtin's notion of heteroglossia – context dependent meaning of words and hybridization – combining different forms of language. From Zolbrod, she notes his two perspectives about double-voice gleaned from Native American literature: a lyrical voice for ceremonial, formal, and sacred aspects of culture and a colloquial or conversational voice for informal storytelling and teaching. Stigter then traces double-voice stylistic features of traditional Indigenous oral stories that current day Indigenous writers use. She indicates that double-voice in Indigenous written stories disappeared during the early post contact times, due to the destructive, oppressive and relentless drive by colonizers to take over of our land, language and culture.

Stigter (2008) shows how contemporary Indigenous writers such as Silko (2006) and Allen (1986), revitalize double-voice and also use another concept of double-consciousness. She attributes the introduction of double-consciousness to William Edward Burghardt Dubois (1903) the first African American to receive a Ph.D. from Harvard University in 1896. Dubois developed this theory in relation to how African American people living in a predominant Euro-American society viewed themselves as; always looking at one's self through the eyes of others.

The bi-cultural nature of contemporary Indigenous writers as noted above and Indigenous scholars cited in this thesis and those such as me are using both traditional double-voice and double-consciousness. With the latter, we are not only viewing ourselves as how others might view us, we are critiquing this world view and examining critically the historical, political, social, economic, and educational issues Indigenous people face as a result of the colonial encounter. I return to *Nlakapmux* stories to illustrate this theory of double-voice and double-consciousness.

I agree with the characterization that the complex and rich stylistic communicative features of *Nlakapmux* oral stories range from the formal ceremonial voice to the colloquial storytelling voice. As an *Nlakapmux* woman who speaks my mother tongue, these *Nlakapmux* forms of story communication are part of my natural "voicing" ways and I know which form is used best in any given cultural situation. However, I have also learned to use the English language, but not without its difficulties.

I am aware that I use this double-voice when I speak in the *Nlakapmuxcin* language: I use ceremonial and storytelling ways of communication. I use the English language and enact double-consciousness when talking about the impact of colonization on our people. I now choose to see an advantage as a bi-cultural person and have learnt to use these techniques from both languages.

My thesis examines how I have confronted this double-consciousness and "looked at myself through my own eyes and the eyes of others." I examined this consciousness through various lenses: my schooling in English, the intimate knowledge of my own language and its use of storywork, calling on genuine sources of knowledge in the form of storywork-based interviews with family members and Elders, and the scrutiny of official records and insightful extrapolation of their content and the exploration of First Nation literature, including work from authors from my own Tribe.

The most important part of my thesis is not only to affirm and demonstrate my own ability to "look at myself through my own eyes and the eyes of others," but through my research goal to identify grandmothers' pedagogy that will assist in learning and teaching environments where new generations of our young people are also able to "look at themselves through their own eyes." The next section presents an overview of the thesis structure.

1.9 Thesis Chapter Descriptions

Chapter 2, *Methodology*, opens with a brief introduction to emerging Indigenous research methodology and continues with a description of my *Nlakapmux* Grandmother's Methodology that includes a *Spilahem* story of my life history, which draws upon Archibald's Indigenous storywork (2008); an analysis of historical and contemporary literature about the *Nlakapmux*; and interviews and circle talks with 11 *Nlakapmux* Grandmothers. The Plains Medicine Wheel and *Nlakapmux* cedar root basket making are used for the wholistic analysis framework.

Chapter 3, *Nchawa Spilahem*: *My Story* introduces my origins and my family going back to the1850's. I tell *Spilahem* stories about my life experiences in my childhood, adult years, and Elderhood. The outward expansion of my world through early travels and forms of conscientization and coming of age are included.

Chapter 4, *Outsider and Insider Stories about the Nlakapmux*, focuses on an analysis of early historical documentation about the *Nlakapmux* as seen through the eyes and perspectives of early ethnographers and outsiders and contemporary Indigenous scholars' representations of *Nlakapmux* culture and stories. This chapter also serves as a literature review.

Chapter 5, *Nlakapmux Grandmother Voices,* shows my analysis and findings of the Grandmothers' perspectives. The chapter opens with an introduction to the participants in my research. I then describe the findings using the Medicine Wheel realms of the physical, mental, emotional, and spiritual areas. Cedar root basket making is used as an *Nlakapmux* metaphor to further refine my findings that are connected to the *Nlakapmux* concept, to live a good life, which is the common message of the Grandmother participants.

Chapter 6, *Caustem (Using) Nlakapmux Pedagogy and Praxis* continues with the analysis and findings process. I weave together the Grandmothers' concepts, teachings, and learnings; my understandings that I acquired in response to the major research questions; and applicable literature to create an *Nlakapmux Developing Wisdom Theory.* This pedagogical theory includes the following eight *Nlakapmux* transformational principles:

- *Takemshooknooqua*, Knowing we are connected: land, animals, plants and people;
- *ChaaChawoowh*, Celebrating people and land joyously;
- *Huckpestes*, Developing lifelong learning and wisdom;
- Huztowaahh, Giving lovingly to family and community;
- *Choownensh*, Succeeding in endeavours;
- *Choowaachoots*, Utilizing Nlakapmux vision-seeking methods;
- *Nmeenlth coynchoots*, Incorporating Nlakapmux knowledge; and
- *Peteenushem*, Reflecting on learning and relearning lifelong lessons.

Chapter 7, *Waasheet/Beginning a New Journey* presents a summary of my research goals, the significance and contribution of the research, its strengths and limitations, its potential applications, and suggestions for future research directions drawing on the research knowledge gained from *Nlakapmux* Grandmothers' stories and their pedagogies. I close this chapter with my personal reflections on carrying out the *Nlakapmux Developing Wisdom Theory* and share one Grandmother's new *Speta'kl* story.

Chapter Two: Methodology

2.1 Introduction to Indigenous Research

Before 1990, research pertaining to Aboriginal people and their communities was often conducted by non-Aboriginals that also reflected Western academic ideology (Chrisjohn, Young, & Maraun, 1997; Vedan, 2002). During the later 1990's, Indigenous graduate students at the doctoral level began to critique and adapt Western methodologies; as well, they introduced and used culturally relevant methodologies (Archibald, 1997; Calliou, 1996; G. Smith, 1997; L.Smith, 1998; Sterling, 1997). Research that appeared in academic journals also began to change. In British Columbia an example of a research shift began with the colloborative research efforts of Dr. Jo-Ann Archibald and Elder Ellen White who documented *Kwulasulwut Syuth, Ellen White's teachings* (1992). This is an example where the Indigenous Elder becomes a lead researcher and author of a research article, instead of a collaborator and participant.

The trend to decolonize Western research methodologies, the theories that inform them, the questions they generate and the writing styles they employ gained momentum as Indigenous scholars contributed to Indigenous knowledge the world over. Various scholars have brought the discourse of Indigenous knowledge into global contexts: Marie Battiste and Sacej Henderson (2000); Marlene Brant Castellano (2000); Gregory Cajete (1994); Sandy Grande (2004); Graham Smith (2003); and Linda Smith (1999). Lester Irbranna Rigney (1999), an Indigenous scholar from the *Narungga* Nation, Australia, affirms that Indigenous people's interests, knowledge and experiences must be at the center of their research methodologies and construction of knowledge about Indigenous people. Increasing numbers of Indigenous graduate students and scholars are developing and using Indigenous Knowledge, Indigenous theories, and Indigenous methodologies (Brown, 2005; Kovach, 2010; Marsden, 2005). Scholars noted above who describe and identify Indigenous worldviews, knowledges, theories and methodologies as valid and important areas within academe are a welcome relief to me, a currently enrolled graduate student.

The scholarship of authors such as Cajete (1994), Chrisjohn (1997), Gardner (2000), Archibald (2008), Sterling (2002) and Cohen (2009) gave me courage to utilize the concepts/theories embedded in my Indigenous language, *Nlakapmuxcin,* for my research. The aforementioned authors have written about Indigenous language, cultural, and political matters based in their cultural contexts; therefore, I am mindful that their contexts have both similarities and differences to mine. I can learn from their challenges and successes but I need to make my approach contextually respectful, relevant, and responsible. The insight I have developed about Indigenous research is that it is varied, diverse, and is unique to the Indigenous people conducting and receiving the research.

I use a narrative, storytelling approach that aims to facilitate healing from colonization and to mobilize Indigenous traditional knowledge advocated by Linda Tuhiwai Smith in her book *Decolonizing Methodologies* (1999). The word "narrative" is used in some places as an alternative to the word "story", as the former connotes a potential of the discovery and development of personal identity, that influeces one's actions (Diaute & Lightfoot, 2004, p. 6). Other scholars also suggest that Indigenous scholarship has elements conducive to the restoration of Indigenous languages, traditions and cultural practices as a means to regain physical, psychological and spiritual health and to empower the cultivation of economic, social and governing Indigenous systems. For example, Cheryl Crazy Bull's scholarship (1997) reinforced my decision to follow Indigenous traditions. Bull states that the goals of Indigenous methodologies are to restore traditions, languages and cultural practices; to revitalize and to regain balance in economic, social and governing systems; and to maintain sovereignty; all of which are relevant to me. This chapter presents my Indigenous approach to research, an *Nlakapmux* Grandmother's methodology. I describe its components, then discuss how the research was carried out, and conclude with information about my analytical framework.

2.2 An *Nlkapmux* Grandmother's Methodology

My research examines how *Nlakapmux* Grandmothers carry out their responsibilities to convey educational and socio-cultural knowledge to grandchildren, family and the community. I use the academic term 'pedagogy' to examine ways that they transmit their knowledge to others. The term 'pedagogy' shows the inextricable link between lifelong teachings and how the learner becomes teacher and vice versa. I also illustrate concepts from the selected use of my mother tongue, the *Nlakapmuxcin* language, to describe meanings that are derived from the Grandmothers' talk and stories. I explain these *Nlakampux* concepts using the English language, which is my second language. In a later chapter, I will elaborate on the difficulties I exerienced with this bilingual approach. I am fortunate to be a fluent *Nlakapmuxcin* speaker. The majority of the Grandmother participants were fluent to somewhat fluent *Nlakapmuxcin* speakers, which made our talks lively, funny, and deep.

The methodology for this thesis includes three major components. First, a self study method incorporates an autobiographical/life history approach that is presented as my story or *Spilaham* (telling/teaching current story) in Chapter Three. This approach examines my life experiences such as how I was taught various things by my parents, grandparents and Elders; how I have been influenced by both traditional and colonial life ways; and how I became conscious of understanding the timeless value of *Nlakapmux*/Indigneous knowledge, especially in my coming of age as an Elder. The memories of the teachings of my childhood were transferred by my Grandmothers, who had stories for correct behaviour, generosity, celebrations and education. My *Spilahem* includes life phases such as my early childhood, public schooling, adulthood, and eldership that address the concept of balance, which is integral to "living a good life." There were times in my life that I was not in balance, which are lessons too. Over the years, I had many conversations with my mother, Mary Anderson, who lived to be 100 years old. Her stories became part of my *Spilahem*. My life stories are shared in a storytelling approach that is guided by Archibald's storywork (2008). Storytelling is consistent with traditional *Nlakapmux* ways of sharing, teaching, knowing and being. I believe that I embody my *Nlakapmux* ways of knowing and inherent knowledge transmission methods and therefore, I tell parts of my life story that are pertinent to the goals of my research and use this type of storytelling as part of my methodology.

A second component of the research methodology is a brief analysis of literature about *Nlakapmux* people as seen from the outsider 'eyes' and perspectives of early ethnographers, James Teit and Franz Boas. Unearthing the historical literature is complex and demands a critical examination of what 'others' said and what they left out about Indigenous people. I appreciated finding stories, songs, and photos from *Nlakapmux* ancestors that I would not have otherwise known about if I had not been doing historical research. To gain an understanding of how insider *Nlakampux* people represent our knowledge and culture in the literature, I turned to the published work of *Nlakampux* community members, Annie York, Darwin Hanna, Mamie Henry, and Shirley Sterling. This review of literature about and by *Nlakapmux* people forms Chapter Four.

A third methodological component includes individual interviews and a circle talks (focus group) meeting with 11 *Nlakapmux* Grandmothers of my extended family network and community that were conducted from January 2009 to September 2010. Cultural protocols were followed to obtain their stories. I gave a gift of tea, jam, tobacco or book in recognition of their participation. I also sought agreement from the Chief of the Band in order to conduct the research in

Nlakapmux territory. My personal preparations through prayer asked for co-operation and successful work each time I invited participation. I followed up with a thank you prayer upon the conclusion of each interview. UBC ethical approval was also secured. The key question that is explored in the semi-structured and open-ended individual interviews was: What and how did your Grandmothers teach you things? The interview questions are listed in Appendix 1.

Information about the Grandmothers' genealogies is an integral part of this research. I examined archival baptismal documents and grave headstones for background information about them. I noticed that the place of baptism is the Reserve Name as they were known then in our families, in this case the *Pekyst/Pokaist* and *Peymanoos Indian Reserves*. These are the reserves where I grew up and these names are still in use today. Personal traditional names anchored individuals' physical, mental, psychological and spiritual identities along with their connection to place. Changing traditional Indigenous names to English ones was systematized by the Churches, contributing further to the erosion of identity and self-determination. For example, my three Great-grandmothers *Lamiinak, Tiila* and *Timlapenak*, all baptized in 1877, had

Nlakapmux names, but during baptism they were given their English names: Jane, Beatrice and Lucy.

The following sections focus on the specifics of my methodology such as storywork, participant selection, carrying out the individual interviews and circle talks (focus group), and analysis framework.

2.3 Storywork

Sto:lo scholar, *Q'um Q'um Xiiem* , Jo-ann Archibald's (2008) *Indigenous Storywork* influenced my research methodology in a number of ways. I was first drawn to Archibald's Storywork methodology because of her conversational storytelling style. I experienced another connection to her scholarship when she used the metaphor of weaving a cedar basket to illustrate the designs or seven storywork principles of respect, responsibility, reverence, reciprocity, wholism, inter-relatedness, and synergy. I thought that the process of weaving cedar baskets and the special meaning of designs resonated with cedar root baskets in my geographical area. The designs on the cedar root baskets can symbolize significant teachings of the woman weaving it. The process of learning to make meaning from and with Indigenous stories based on the storywork principles seemed like a non-threatening way with which to work with *Nlakapmux* Grandmothers' stories.

The two major genres of *Nlakapmux* stories, *Spilahem,* which connotes a 'personal telling' of lived experiences and reflects current times, and *Speta'kl,* which are Creation and past/traditional stories, are presented in my research. I learn to make my own *Nlakapmux* storywork basket with its unique designs, which are discussed in Chapter Six. An additional insight is that my effort to use a new concept like 'storywork' is akin to a new use of a *Nlakapmux* traditional concept of *Shinkyap* /Coyote. Archibald mentions that Coyote became her critical friend during her research journey. Throughout my methodology *Shinkyap* was my constant companion that prodded me to reflect, imagine, and create story understandings. At times in this thesis *Shinkyap* takes on the role of teacher to help us understand Grandmothers' pedagogy.
Having an Indigenous methodological framework to guide me was helpful. Archibald (2008) reminds us to develop respectful relations with those from whom we learn (research participants), to learn responsible protocols associated with stories, to acknowledge spirit/reverence towards stories and story listeners/learners, and to share/give back in order to keep the power of Indigenous Knowledge and Indigenous stories alive and strong. The principles

of wholism, inter-relatedness, and synergy help us understand and appreciate the nature of Indigenous stories (epistemology) and how to make meaning with and through them (pedagogy). In the spirit of sharing and giving back, I show next how I carried out the storywork principles of respect, responsibility, reverence, and reciprocity. In the analysis discussion below the principles of wholism, inter-relatedness, and synergy are enacted.

2.3.1 Respect

I showed respect to my interviewees by honouring them with a small gift when we met. I was mindful of their time spent and made sure they were not rushed. I did not interupt them as they were speaking. I clarified by repeating what I heard when necessary. I did not stop the Elder when she had digressed to talk of family lineages. I then rephrased the question in our language after she had finished speaking. Similarily, with others who wandered off topic, I heard what they were sharing then rephrased or restated the question.

2.3.2 Responsibility

In this area, I demonstrated responsibility by being on time for the interviews and group discussions and clarified the time I needed for my questions. I made sure that the Grandmothers were clear about what I was doing. I asked them for their contribution and did not keep them beyond the time agreed upon for each visit.

2.3.3 Reverence

I showed reverence for their contribution by thanking them for their contribution and also in the group setting we engaged in prayer, smudging and sharing a meal.

2.3.4 Reciprocity

I plan to give 'back' to my participants a hard copy of my thesis. The local Band library will also receive a copy so that *Nlakapmux* current and future community members can access this research.

2.4 Participant Selection

In order to address my major research questions (see Chapter One), I focussed on one *Nlakapmux* family (mine) in order to gain an understanding of the female family members' intergenerational perspectives. The selection of *Nlakapmux* Grandmothers includes five of my siblings, one niece, and my daughter. Originally, I was not going to include family members who were not my siblings. But as news of my interviews circulated in my family and the community, my niece and daughter wished to be involved because they believed that they had significant *Nlakapmux* teachings from their great-Grandmother and Grandmother. Therefore in keeping with our tradition of inclusion they were included in my research. They are also Grandmothers. Four generations of the Anderson family from Spences Bridge are represented in my research. In addition, four other *Nlakapmux* community Grandmothers were included to gain a broader community understanding of Grandmothers' teachings. The *Nlakapmux* community involved in this study is located near Spence's Bridge and Merritt in the Interior of British Columbia. The families selected have fluent *Nlakapmux* speakers who have continued to pass down cultural knowledge to their family members and their community. All the Grandmother participants are *Nlakapmux* but not all are *Nlakapmux* speakers. Only three of us are fluent speakers and all others have an awareness and response to *Nlakapmuxcin*. The Grandmother voices are introduced in Chapter Five.

I first sent an e-mail to each Grandmother who had e-mail (7) informing her of my study and asking her to consider being involved in it. I then followed up by sending her a hard copy letter and phoned her to provide additional information as necessary. For the other four Grandmothers, I phoned for an appointment and asked if I could come and talk to them about my study and asked for their involvement in person. I obtained verbal permission to record each Grandmother prior to setting up the interview and then obtained their signed consent letters at the conclusion of the interview. Each Grandmother was enthusiastic about my study and readily agreed to participate. Their family's private homes were used for the individual interviews. Family protocols were identified in our initial talks about participating in the research and they were carried out during the interviews. For example, one of my siblings, after starting the interview, asked to postpone the interview for a few days, to get ready. She wanted to think about the questions some more before engaging in the process. In one of the Elder Grandmother's interviews we stopped, while a family member visited. Another Grandmother asked to go for tea in the middle of the interview, we did so. All those who participated consented to the use of their *Nlakapmux* and English names.

At the beginning of the interview, I informed each Grandmother that anything we discussed would be used for research purposes and subsequently written and shared in a public document available through the university. I asked permission to tape record our conversation so that I would not miss any of their ideas. I mentioned that the interview transcript would be filed with my advisor as required by UBC ethics but that she would honour their confidentiality as noted in the letter of informed consent. I also said that I would get their approval of what they said in the transcript and the thesis. They were given time to ask me any questions before we started the interview. Each person was encouraged to ask any questions or add comments at any time during our time together.

All of the grandmothers were interviewed on an individual basis for one hour to three hours. There were some challenges to locate space and time for the interviews, however the biggest challenges were with the older Grandmothers. For example, the structured interview question and answer process proved unworkable as the older Grandmother would lapse into storytelling mode of kinship lines and histories, regardless of my attempts to re-direct the conversation. To show respect, I allowed the conversation to emerge, letting this Grandmother determine what we talked about during our time together. After the interview, I felt nervous because I was not sure how to make meaning of her talk and her stories. However, after much reflection, I realized that she wanted to emphasize the importance of knowing our relatives, in effect, to help us know who comprised our extended kinship in our *Nlakampux* families and communities. In Chapter Five and Six, the implications of family and community and the idea of knowing our kinship that helped to shape these ideas are discussed. My experience of interviewing this particular Grandmother reminded me of Cruikshank's experience with learning to let her research participants who were Indigenous Elders determine the direction of their talks (1990).

I learned to let the other interviews with the Grandmothers evolve spontaneously, and, as the interview progressed, it became conversational in nature with more of the *Nlakapmuxcin* language emerging with the fluent speakers. The questions that guided our discussions included: What were the things your Grandmothers taught you? How did they teach you these things? How have these teachings changed over the years and what aspects if any are useful today? How have Grandmothers' teachings and ways of teaching helped grandchildren live a good life, traditionally and today? The interview with the eldest Grandmother who was 84 was conducted mostly in the *Nlakapmuxcin* language. It was difficult for me to transcribe the interviews in which *Nlakapmuxcin* was spoken. I am not a linguist nor do I use the written form or orthography that others who teach *Nlakapmuxcin* have developed. I listened to these tapes many times to ensure that I captured correctly the Grandmother's concepts, ideas, and perspectives told in *Nlakapmuxcin*.

After the interview transcripts were verified with participants and after I had completed an initial round of analysis, I organized circle talks (focus groups) to authenticate my findings with the participants. I call these 'circle talks' because we sat in a circle and observed the Talking Circle protocol of speaking one at a time, without interrupting one another. These talks were also an opportunity for the Grandmothers to add new thoughts or remembrances. These sessions were held on September 11th and 18th 2010 in Merritt, BC, because the older Grandmothers lived in the area and it was easier for them to meet near to their homes. Each session was two hours long and attended by most of the Grandmothers with five participants at the September 11th session and six participants at the September 18th session.

I opened each circle talk with a prayer and smudge of sacred plants. We then made time for a check-in where each person could talk about how she was feeling and anything else that she wanted to talk about. A check-in is useful for bringing everyone up to date about their trip or what is currently happening in their lives. Then I gave a presentation of my preliminary interview findings. I had categorized my findings on a flip chart and noted how many common responses there had been, arranging them in four categories of the Medicine Wheel: physical, emotional, mental and spiritual spheres. They were encouraged to share and add thoughts as they arose during the conversations. I recorded the Grandmothers' comments on the flip chart.

During our talk, I shared that although the Medicine Wheel had been my previous choice to illustrate their perspectives, I wanted to use an *Nlakapmux* metaphor and model to illustrate this research. I shared my idea of using of the Cedar Root Basket to illustrate my findings. Many of the Grandmothers had talked about learning to make baskets in their interviews. When they heard of the Cedar Root Basket as a metaphor, they were excited. The older Grandmothers said the cedar root basket-making was a hard task. Another said she had not seen anyone make a basket since she was very young. One of the Grandmothers, who has a master's degree, said she thought it was very appropriate and made a comparison between making a basket and making a thesis. After two hours of circle sharing we concluded the sharing circle by asking for a safe journey prayer for all of us and for the work that we had completed. We enjoyed food together. Each circle talk was conducted the same way with several of the Grandmothers being present for both talks, which resulted in richer feedback. The circle talks helped me to refine the analysis process and to act as a catalyst for the findings' framework.

2.5 Analysis

The transcriptions of the 11 participants' conversations were analyzed through a process involving several steps. I began by sorting their descriptions of experiences, stories and recollections and examining them for common word usage. Based on their usage frequency, these words were then prioritized. A number of categories/themes emerged from what was most important and several procedures were then employed to examine the commonalities. For example, *Nlakapmux* knowledge transmission occurred in the following ways: participating in ceremonies such as puberty ceremonies, observation of role models, story-telling of Grandmothers, sharing of a work activity, and carrying out daily practices.

I sorted experiences, ideas, and concepts according to physical, emotional, mental and spiritual teachings of the Medicine Wheel. I believe that the Medicine Wheel is conducive to the restoration of Indigenous languages, traditions and cultural practices as a means to regain wholistic health and to empower the cultivation of personal growth and wellness. I adapted the Medicine Wheel framework of Lane, Bopp, Bopp, & Brown (1983), which was one of the first such frameworks to be published. I have based my understanding of wholism on *Nlakapmux* good life teachings. I linked each realm with four major life phases and the cardinal directions: physical with childhood in the southern direction; spiritual with Elderhood in the northern direction; emotional with youth in the western direction; and mental with adulthood in the eastern direction. I explain my meaning of the Medicine Wheel framework in Chapter Five.

Because I wanted this research to truly reflect *Nlakampux* knowledge and ways of knowing, I turned to an *Nlakapmux* traditional form of women's work to refine my analysis: cedar root basket making (see Chapters Five and Six). In the section above I described how the Grandmothers' reaction in circle talks encouraged me to use cedar root basket making as another framework analysis. During the analysis process I experienced the following Indigenous storywork principles that Archibald advocates: understanding the wholistic nature of stories and making meaning in this way; appreciating the inter-relatedness of Indigenous teachings embedded in the stories; and experiencing the power of synergy when participants begin to share their ideas and then build upon each other's so that the ideas, teachings, and story meanings become deeper and more meaningful.

2.6 Summary

My thesis research is situated in the qualitative realm of research. However, I moved from qualitative methodology to develop an Indigenous Grandmother's methodology where I use storywork (Archibald, 2008) and life history; examine historical records; talk with Grandmothers; and apply an Indigenous analysis framework based on wholism and an *Nlakapmux* metaphor of cedar root basket making.

I agree with the approaches of Indigenous researchers who were mentioned in the opening section of this chapter and who are mindful and sensitive to their ethical and cultural accountabilities as researchers and storytellers. We, as Indigenous reserachers, are given a wonderful opportunity to reclaim our self-determination in documenting and presenting our cultural knowledge and most importantly we become witnesses and learners as we listen to participants' stories that present their realities of Indigenous lives, their aspirations, their languages, and their timeless teachings. Indigenous scholar Michael Marker reinforces the value of research conducted from an Indigenous methodology:

> These approaches connect and draw from Indigenous knowledge and privilege Indigenous pedagogies in their practices, relationships and methodologies. Most Indigenous researchers would claim that their research validates an ethical and culturally defined approach that enables

Indigenous communities to theorize their own lives and that connects their past histories with their future lives (Marker, 2003, p.4).

To develop and carry out my Indigenous Grandmother's methodology, I drew upon my bi-cultural nature, portraying my research from a rich First Nations cultural domain that is rooted in a life lived, especially in my early years, exclusively in orality, and embedded in *Nlakapmux* Knowledge and the *Nlakapmuxcin* language. I am also a graduate student, a social worker, and an instructor who also lives in the Western world of academe and education. In order to exist in these worlds, I am like *Shinkyap,* who takes on shape-shifter, transformer roles in bringing these various worldviews together in a research context. Even though we live in a contemporary world, we are intimately connected to our past. *Shinkyap* is the thread that binds us. In the past of long ago, we imprinted our stories and thoughts using symbols carved onto stone (petroglyphs) and symbols painted on stone(pictographs). Today we imprint our stories and ideas using the symbols of the English letters onto paper pages that others call a thesis. In doing this work various ethical considerations arise.

I adhered to Indigenous protocols and met the university's ethical and documentation practices. The research/data records are kept in a format that is acceptable to the faculty advisors and my research participants, the

Grandmothers. However, from an Aboriginal point of view, there are also other ethical issues to consider. One important example is the ownership of personal story knowledge. I believe that this type of knowledge belongs to each research participant; therefore, I credit each grandmother for her stories and they remain the property of each individual Grandmother and her family[3].

[3] I am aware of issues about appropriation and intellectual property rights (Battiste & Henderson, 2000; Young-Ing, 2006) regarding Indigenous stories and Indigenous Knowledge, which is why it was important for me to ensure that each Grandmother maintained ownership of her knowledge and stories. Each Grandmother's quotes are attributed to her for those who wish to follow academic protocol of using quotes and naming/acknowledging the Grandmother for her stories/words in other publications.

Chapter Three: *NCHAWA SPILAHEM*: My Story

To be true to my *Nlakapmux* teachings I must first tell my story to give readers an understanding of who I am and to introduce examples of Grandmother pedagogy. The purpose of telling my story which follows is to provide a framework of how I, an *Nlakapmux* Grandmother, arrived to the place where I am, passing down my story as a form of intergenerational Indigenous knowledge content. In *Nlakapmux* oral tradition, we tell people about our origins, our ancestors, and we share our experiences that have significantly shaped who we are.

In accordance with *Nlakapmux* tradition my story begins with my Grandmother *Tiilaa* (1870-1957), daughter of *Semxelc'e* (1845-1908) (Living Spirit) and Kamenccnak (Sara) one of (twelve children residing in *Ngaggh* (Dry Creek, *Inkuku* Creek, Toketic) near Spence's Bridge, British Columbia. I grew up on our land-holding there. It is now called Indian Reserve # 9 (*Peymanoos*). It was a land space and place going back to my great, great grandfather's time in the 1800's situating my family there, from baptismal records of the Anglican Church. We know that my great grandfather's S*emxelc'e* baptism occurred on June 1, 1873, and his children were all baptized Anglicans in the 1870's. My

Great-great grandfather was renamed Timothy (*Semxelc'e*). The following photograph and map (Figure 2) depict my family and land roots.

Figure 2. *Semxelc'e* and Kamenccnak Family and Territory

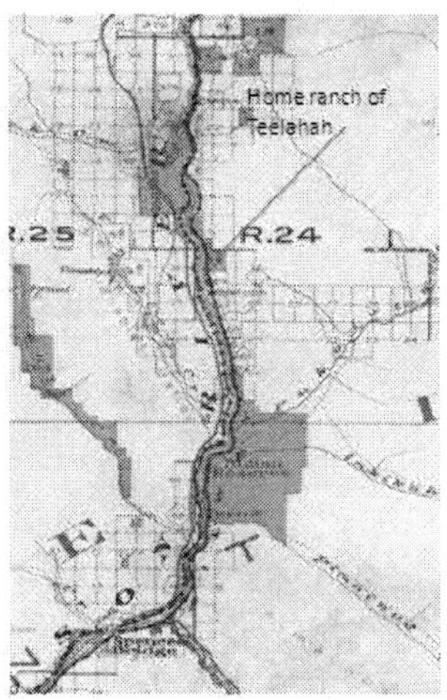

Disease and destiny placed my father in his Grandaunt's (*Tiilaa*, Beatrice Anderson) care. She was a daughter of Chief *Semxelc'e*, who was also known as Timothy *Shemahallsee*. In the latter part of the nineteenth century, Timothy *Shemahallsee* was the Chief at *Pekeyst (Pokaist, Pakyst*) on the east bank of the Thompson River. *Tiilaa*, Beatrice was his surrogate mother and her husband William Henry Anderson was his father. *Tiilaa* had already raised an only daughter Isabella Minnabarriet (1894-1931) who had married and left with a railroad worker, a Swede, named Swan Johnson. They had one daughter, Lily, and one son named Carl. Isabella had been her only child from the son of a settler Louis Minnabarriet with roots from Basque, Spain. Later, she and

William Anderson, a 'half breed' with an *Nlakapmux* mother, had no biological children but following the custom of the tribe they adopted her great nephew, Jacob, my father (see Figure 2 above).

The records show *Semxelc'e* had two wives, in his lifetime and eleven children, and it is known that he adopted a twelfth child, Nancy Minnabarriet. Six children, Arthur, Henry, Laura, John, Amy and Ethel, were listed in the parish records in the 1870's, but they were not identified in subsequent records. Two other sons, Moses and Albert, also do not appear in the records. The children who are remembered well are his three younger daughters, Jane (*Lamiinak*), Beatrice (*Tiilaa*) and Lucy (*Timilpinek*), and his adopted daughter Nancy. Jane was the mother of Ann Drynock and William Patterson and grandmother of Jacob Anderson. Beatrice adopted Jacob as an infant after the death of his parents, and raised him as her son. Nancy who married Louis Minnabarriet is the grandmother to Percy Minnabarriet. Although *Semxelc'e* had his principal residence at *Pekyst*, his family also lived at *Nkxkix, Tookitti* and *Xeweiskn*, two nearby villages and his other descendants lived across the river at *S'mgew. Semxelc'e* was the brother of *Ntl'qi*'; therefore he was the uncle of *Titl'nice*

(Tetlneetsa /tattered robe), the Chief of the Spence's Bridge Band in the early 1900's and a friend and advisor of James Teit.

There are many people who appear in the early parish records as members of the *Semxelc'e* House. They were members of the extended family. The graves at *Pekyst* also include James *Shelza* whose position in the family is now unknown. There were other people living in *Pekyst*, women named *Losta'a, Ultquwu, Ti'uy* and *Wewtko*, who were Percy Minnabarriet's great Grandmothers and her sisters. *Semxelc'e* died in 1908 and is buried in the *Pekyst* graveyard. His wife Kamenccnak (Sara) died in 1887, the year Lucy, *Timlipenek*, his youngest daughter was born.

It was Granny *Tiilaa* who told me stories of the hard times and many changes the people endured. She described new influences, such as the surveyors, and mapping land, Indian agents bringing rules and church people, men in black robes with little books, preaching to them in their homes and eventually building churches in their territories. She did not tell me explicitly of her or my father's conversion to Christianity. When my father was ten or eleven the Residential School in Lytton was taking children for their education, Granny and Grandpa decided their only son, Jacob, would stay home.

Granny and Grandpa raised Jacob, my father, on 40 acres of arid land, thriving under their constant effort to irrigate and raise hay and cattle. Daybreak to nightfall was filled with chores on the farm, unceasingly demanding their time, summer and winter alike. Their agricultural work included long hours toiling to grow food and raise animals. The river people not having enough land to grow hay for their cattle took them to summer pasture high in the mountains where the grass grew freely in their hunting grounds in the Highland Valley area. The cattle would feed until snowfall. They would return to the riverbanks and the farm where they were fed from hay stacks put up in summer time. I remember Granny saying it was this work in the high mountains of the Highland Valley, which kept father from being found and removed to Residential School by the school police. I grew up with the knowledge that the *Indian Act* had been used to take children away and forced to attend Residential School.

By the 1930's, father was 19 years old and thriving. Eager to seek his fortune, he rode the rails to Vancouver and also to Alberta, only to find poverty and hunger everywhere. After seeing this devastation he returned home to the reservation and food aplenty on the farm where the old folks carried on their farming activities as before. During his twenties father settled down, helping on the farm, and working as a casual labourer on the Canadian Pacific Railroad

(CPR). When opportunity came, he would cook for the extra gangs when they came to upgrade the ties on the railroad. Mother's story intercepts father's when they became a couple in 1930. Mother was raised only nine miles away on the same railroad line and already had three children from a previously arranged marriage. Only one of these children was to survive; my brother Percy Minnabarriet.

My maternal Grandmother (*Whatpalx,* Clara Edmonds 1872-1949) had raised Mary my mother, her last child. My maternal Grandmother married a younger man working on the railroad, Nicholas (*Toohooshumalst*) Edmonds (1888-1957), who had also driven stage coach from Ashcroft to Spence's Bridge during his youth. While my Grandfather Edmonds was with Granny *Whatpalx,* he worked on the railroad at *Spapttsin* (Spatsum) and toiled the land after hours with Granny to grow produce to eat and hay to feed cattle. They also pastured cows in the Highland Valley area, the meadow high in the mountains, where my parents had met in their childhood: playing together, riding horses and fishing in the lakes in their locale, Fish Lake, Divide Lake, and Little Divide Lake. Mary, like Jacob, escaped the Residential School.

Jacob proposed to Mary in 1929 when he visited her and her mother in their home. Mary told her story of their marriage proposal. "Jacob said, 'I am interested in having a family and would like you to be mother of my children, however I ask that you consider being free from tobacco and alcohol should you wish to do so. I'll return in one year for your answer!" (Herbert, 1994, p.5). Needless to say, she agreed to marry and start a family on those terms; however, it was almost ten years before I was born.

3.1 My Origin

I, Beatrice Marie (*Teelahah*), was born 71 years ago, in 1940 near the small railroad town of Ashcroft in central British Columbia. My home was approximately 25 miles upriver from Ashcroft. I was a tiny girl under six pounds born to parents of *Nlakapmux* (Thompson River-Salish people) origins. I was the fourth birth to my mother and the first to my father. They had lived together for almost ten years. Mother was rendered sterile by *Nlakapmux* herbal medicine taken upon the dissolution of her arranged first marriage and I, an answer to their prayers, was born ten years into their union. For the first seven years of my life I lived exclusively with my parents and grandparents at the home of my ancestors, *Semxelc'e* (Timothy) (1845-1908) at *Ngh-gh* Inkuk, (Dry Creek).

Learnings coming to my mind are the splendid times I enjoyed riding horseback with Great Grandmother *Lamiinak*, behind the saddle, when I became old enough to accompany her when she went Saskatoon berry picking in the summertime. She gave me a little cedar root basket just like hers, and we would have a lunch and a tarp to place on the ground to sit on for the picnic. While picking berries, my Grandmother would pray, sing and laugh and talk about other times, places, relatives and the other people she had picked berries with over the years. She sang as she picked, talking to the berries about what a welcome sight they were and giving thanks to Mother Earth and Grandmother Sun for ripening them. She often asked me to take her little basket to empty into the big basket sitting in the shade of the big lone pine tree where we had shared lunch. I complied willingly as there was never any doubt that I was capable of such a feat and in time when I filled my basket I would also put my berries in the big basket. We would ride back home to clean the berries and place them on *s/zelt-?uy* cattail mats to dry.

Figure 3. My Three Great-Grandmothers

(Tiilaa, Lamiinak, and Alice)

When I was a child, my great-grandmothers, *Tiilaa, Lamiinak*, and Alice , all pictured above, would come to visit often. They would tell us stories and we children had a practice to say "*ayee, ayee*" at intervals to let them know we were listening. I loved to hear the stories they told. Sometimes, *YaYa* (Great-Grandmothers' pet name) would make *shooshum* or soopalalie berries, beaten into foam with a cedar whisk in a big t*cyea,* cedar root basket. She would add *koyush*, a wild plant sweetener, and we would all dig in with spoons until we could eat no more. It is now referred to as Indian Ice-cream, *shwushem*.

Nowadays we also make a liquid concentrate to enjoy this berry as a beverage. Grandfather demonstrated unfailing love and guidance in his quiet, gentle way. He told us stories as we went riding horseback with him to irrigate the fields and then watch the water, to ensure it ran in the correct little rows he had dug for them, or we would go looking for the cattle on horseback away up in the mountains, all the time keeping an eye out for bees among the trees. This was such an exciting time. When we found the bees, he would remember the spot and say he would return on a rainy day. On the decided day he would bring several big cedar root baskets, some sagebrush, and matches too, along on horseback to the remembered spot. After he arrived home with the honeycombs, Grandmother *Tiilaa* put the combs in big black baking pans into the wood stove oven at a low temperature, the honey would ooze into the pan, smelling of sweet flowers, ready to be poured into the jars.

This golden liquid was always a special treat. Grandmother *Tiilaa* told us the story of how the bees made the honey, how important their work was and how, therefore, we must only take half of the honey, as the bees needed it for their survival in the cold winter months. She told us the honeybee would travel over a mile for nectar and always went back to the same tree hive to deposit the nectar gathered. She marveled at the skill of the bee to make honey, being such a tiny creature. She also shared that the rainy day and the smoke were insurance against stings and was necessary for the successful harvesting of this delicious sweet. Reflecting on this form of Indigenous Knowledge, I noticed that questions were answered when asked, not delaying but telling us when we were enjoying the sweet. Grandmother *Tiilaa* practiced personal experiential teaching, imprinting the lesson of bee collecting, harvesting and enjoyment in my living memory.

The memories of this period in my life were carefree and safe and snug in the knowledge that mom would be home with a new baby very soon. Since I grew up on a small land holding on the reserve my immediate family received periodic visits from my numerous uncles and other travelers who went by our house journeying to town for food or going somewhere else. During those days, I remember that if someone came by, *Yaya* (*Tiilaa*-granny) immediately made tea and began to cook something. She never asked the visitors if they wanted to eat with us. She just did it as a practice of hospitality, and invariably we had another place to set for dinner or lunch. Anyone riding by on horseback was invited for a cup of tea and a meal.

I remember an elderly blind man, who lived about two miles away, being a regular visitor. He was a bachelor and he came around at least once a week or so it seemed, I cannot say with any certainty, however, now in hindsight, I could have counted the times he visited by the number of dimes he gave to me and my sister after each time he ate. My sister and I had baking powder tins full of dimes, which only he had given us every time he stopped for a meal. In fact he was the only person who offered us dimes and who loved to tease us children with stories and jokes about his horse Barney. He talked about Barney as if he were a personal friend of his, thanking him for carrying him around the country trails to our house.

My grandmother also told me of the Whip Man. She said that long ago, when people still lived in their *sheestkens,* or winter (pit) houses and when the ice and snow were melted in early spring, the traditional practice was to assemble all the children outside their homes and await the arrival of the Whip Man who made his rounds to administer a whipping with a long willow stick. Only the Grandmother could intervene, by lifting her skirts and taking the whipping on behalf of her grandchild if she felt the whipping to be unwarranted. I also remember Grandmother, *Lamiinak.* I was her favorite because I was the eldest; she had carried me around in a sling on her back from one to two years old. She spoke of this practice and I always felt she would intervene on my behalf if Whip Man were to suddenly appear.

My earliest awareness was of prayers being said by my Grandmother at nightfall and during the day, when picking berries or fishing at the river. It was also commonplace to say prayers before eating and before traveling. While growing up one of my favorite times was when Granny *Tiilaa* made soapberry ice-cream foam of the bitter berry with sugar to sweeten it, made in a mixing bowl and whipped by an egg beater. We would all sit around with tablespoons, going to the creek to drink water when we felt stuffed as it had that property to fill you with foam. Later, when we all went to bed in the house, we all slept in one room with a bed in each corner to begin with granny and grandpa in one corner, mom and dad in the other corner and myself and my sister in another corner.

As the other children were born we slept three to the bed in the other corner then in another two beds between the corners, in our old log house, with wood plank floors and a potbellied stove. Our log house had a tar paper roof and by today's standards was a very poor house; however, I always felt very safe and secure there, as I drifted off to sleep with either Granny or Grandpa telling us a story about coyote, owl, grizzly bear or crow or chipmunk. Sometimes it would be mom and dad talking about the day and tomorrow's activities. We lived in this little house until I was seventeen. It was not a solitary life as I had seven siblings as all the neighbor children had been taken to Residential School. It was happy days when they came home for holidays, coming to play and share their experiences about school, singing hymns and singing cowboy songs.

Another neighbor, Pearl B, was a close friend. While growing up we rode horse back all over the ranch and the reserve, racing our horses and going to the old swimming hole in the summer time. She loved me so much she earned money to buy me a very fancy dress, which I wore once, on the occasion of my marriage at the age of 21.

3.2 Early Memories of Travel and Schooling

The area I was raised in was the Central Interior of the province known for its aridness and heat in summertime. I remember the expansion of my circle came when mother would take me to town. First, we would bathe in the old round galvanized tub and then get dressed in town clothes. I would ride behind her on horseback, then we would go to a little place, a shed, the size of an outhouse, by the railroad track, where a white flag was stored to flag the passenger train to stop for us. We then would board the train for a short ride to the town for shopping in the country store for food. I got acquainted with the brakeman who helped us board the train, then the conductor took our quarters for the ride to town; their names were Harry and Laurie.

These men became our uncles even though they were white and new to our family; they did this by bringing us used clothing and greeting us warmly when they swung us into the train. I had frequent sojourns to my aunt's house to attend public school. In my later school years, I traveled alone by train 50 miles away and they cared for me and made sure I dismounted into the arms of my uncle Tommy Hewitt (he was actually my mom's nephew, but I called him uncle as is our custom) with whom I was living until grade six. So gradually I became community oriented in this way. My community was like my immediate family that included my train family and my school community. However, these community family interactions were under the watchful eyes of my parents and grandmothers.

At the age of seven I was taken to a public school. As my parents had eluded Residential School, at first they did not wish me to attend either. I was taken to my Mother's nephew and his family to live in their home in a small community called Walhachin, where he (the nephew) worked for the Canadian Pacific Railroad. To get there I had to ride the train for one hour, and would return home on the weekends. I remember that first year my two grannies came by train to attend the first Christmas school concert. Mom was at the hospital awaiting another sister who was born on Dec 31,1947. Daddy and grandpa stayed home with my three younger sisters. When we got home Granny took over the child minding responsibilities, and this was the year I discovered a dissonance with my younger sisters when they heard me speaking English for the first time.

I remember they said things like, "she is speaking English, she is turning into a *Shamaa*" (whiteman)!! I had been away from them for four months and was missing them terribly. I was so happy to be home, but it was upsetting to be greeted by these comments. I cried, speaking in our language, saying, that now I could speak both languages, however, I felt uneasiness at home for the first time. My childhood was becoming complicated.

School was a foreign environment and all communication was in English and my cousin Harvey, who was two years older, became my constant companion and protector. He fought the kids who called us names like "dirty Indian," and I was bewildered as I was not dirty and I did not know that I was an Indian. My Aunt and Uncle coached their son not to hit our tormentors unless they hit him first and then they said he could hit them if they took the first blow. I remember us going home many times with Harvey bleeding from the nose. I was happy that no one hit me, probably because I was a girl. However, they pushed me and called me names like "Squaw" and taunted us as we walked to and from school. I rode in the back of a pick up truck for the first time to Falkland, over 100 miles to a rodeo at the age of seven.

I grew up in that small town with the one room school until I was in grade six. I became a member of the community, I think, witnessed by my peers as an able playmate to drag our homemade bob-sled seating at least four children, up the hill to slide downhill in the winter time and to go in a group, trick or treating at Halloween. I also remember after supper time beginning in May, we would go to the Thompson River as a family and Uncle Tommy fished for trout for supper the next day. This food activity was a daily occurrence as there was no refrigerator at the time and the fish could only keep overnight and then have to be eaten for supper.

Life changed drastically for me at this time since I was no longer part of the safe environment of my preschool years, but was a guest in my Auntie and Uncle's (Agnes and Thomas Hewitt) home. My mother stayed with me for over one month to help me feel that I was not being abandoned. Yet I did feel abandoned when she left and I knew little alleviation of that feeling for many years. I actually remember when I stopped crying every time I left home on those long ago Sundays. It was one Sunday when I was in grade six, while sitting in my seat in the train looking out the window upon my departure that I noticed my Mother crying too. I pledged that I would not make her cry again. So I stopped crying after saying good-bye. Once again, upon reflection it occurred to me that I did notice and drew a lesson from her tears: it's hurting me too, and so I wanted to alleviate her distress.

3.3 Conscientization, Coming of Age, and Leadership

Sometimes I feel like I am a shape shifter, trying on different shapes and form fitting, feeling like an imposter wanting to fit into each different environment, and sometimes I still feel very much like an imposter. I believe these efforts began when I began formal schooling and found there were others who were not of my culture and had already a negative, painful view of the world, even in a tiny *shama* (white) town of approximately 19 houses. The community offered a basic one-room class and there was one teacher for all the children of mixed heritage that were from grades one to eight.

Up until that time I had been the center of the universe for my parents and grandparents at *Ngaggh* Creek (Dry Creek) and, as children, we were regarded as treasured gifts from the Creator. I remember Father telling us daily that we were all special, beautiful and wanted. I have fond memories of my Grandma *Lamiinak* packing me in her sling on her back going for walks in the hayfields, taking the working men their lunches, so they would not lose time by going in to the house to eat. And later as I became a little older, my father used to take me on his work day packing me around the farm as he performed his chores, irrigating the fields, watering the stock, hauling water for the house and sometimes feeding the hay to the cattle in the winter time. Sometimes, when times allowed we would watch the clouds sail by as if on a movie screen, imagining all kinds of pictures and other scenic Panavision shots. The wind in the trees and the bird sounds in the early evening remain unequaled in my storehouse of memories of my early childhood days.

Our family raised all its own food and cared for one another in a farm setting. When we were in grade seven we rode horses eight miles to school. After grade eight we rowed on the Thompson River before catching the school bus on the way to Ashcroft. My parents did not send us to Residential School as others parents did; we were alone on the Reserve. Thank goodness there were lots of siblings to interact with and of course when our relatives returned from Residential School we had lots of catching up time and sharing our experiences. They sang hymns beautifully and we sang the current nursery rhymes we knew and made up other verses as we sang along. Mother and father taught us to be self-sufficient at an early age, for me being the eldest I quickly became their helper and supporter as we had little material possessions and eight children in all, by the time I was 14. I became an accomplished bread-maker, cook and child minder. I went to school at age seven and found out I was a minority, and different. The other children had different appearances in dress and mannerisms, a few were friendly and some quite rude.

As a child I was influenced greatly by the stories told to me by my great grandmothers, and later learned that father and mother were determined to have a family because they were both an only child. They always told us to wait until we were 30 to have a family at which time we would be mature enough to put our family first, which they did by being a good example, no alcohol or smoking and fresh food and fresh air every day.

No stories were told of early Christianizing efforts by the Anglican Church and the little churches on the reservation were used to baptize children and service the dead during funerals. I used to imagine where people were buried before we had graveyards. So when I asked my Grandmother *Tiilaa*, she told me, in prior times, the dead were buried in a fetal position or under a shale mountain in areas not accessible to wild animals.

Although both my parents never attended school, they saw the value in education and took great pains to make sure I attended. I believe I never missed a school day despite the distances we had to travel, and I read my report card with A's and explained my marks to my mother. I was very good in school. I then signed my mother's name on the back of the card as she instructed me. There were prayers for the food for every meal and other prayers for the ill and missing relatives. My father's struggle for ways to pray were demonstrated in his quest for what religion to follow as his mother reminded him he was not to practice our "pagan" ways because they had been outlawed by the federal government. Nonetheless, he often prayed in our language and read scriptures he encountered aloud, including the work of Mary Baker Eddy, author of

Christian Science journals, the bible and the dictionary to us children and Mother.

During my pubescent days I learned that our cultural ways were in question when my mother asked my Grandmother to teach me the rites of passage. When she refused, my mother cried and showed me what rituals to perform. I was relieved to know that I was merely becoming ready for motherhood and not really dying by the loss of blood. I recall that many teachings were passed along by my Grandmothers that focused on the pursuit of a good life, not causing any damage to the ecology, and to do no harm to the people or the surroundings. The prayers that I remember being said in our language were to take care of nature and nature will take care of you 'forever.' I was taught that our people took only what they needed and that if there was extra they shared what they had with their neighbor or kinfolk. This teaching was demonstrated to me during my childhood, as I grew up on a little farm. My grandparents and parents raised cattle, chickens, turkeys, pigs and plants, vegetables and fruit. Anyone passing by was welcome at our dinner table.

When I accompanied my Grandmother shopping, I recall her telling me that the life of our family began to slowly change with the advent of this major work along the river. Men from the tribe began different work, where life prior to this was spent in hunting, fishing and gathering food. New work brought new currency and new ways of acquiring basic needs. Stores stocked supplies for the railroad workers and others who were settling in the territory, stores brought new utensils to our people. Several sources of information exist describing these early times. We lived in a time of great change, technologically and culturally. First Nations people of my tribe have lived and survived along the Thompson River for centuries prior to the arrival of Anglo-explorers Simon Fraser in 1808 and David Thompson a little later; we were known to our neighbors as the People of the River. " We traded with our neighbors of the four directions to fulfill our daily needs" (personal communication with Grandmother *Tiilaa*, 1955). With the arrival of the European, my paternal grandmother had stories of the sighting of the new first 'White man', a traveler along the river and soon, loud noises, explosions, as the railroad building began. Whenever she and her child relatives heard the loud explosions they would run and hide, not knowing the trans Canada rail line would soon stretch from the Atlantic to Pacific Oceans.

I wanted to marry at the age of 20; however, I had to wait until I became 21, because my parents would not give their consent. I married a fellow from a nearby reserve that was 40 miles away as that was the expectation of the day. We had three children in 1961, 1962 and 1964. In those days I believed in a happily ever after, fairytale style life. However, the custom of the family was to provide for the extended family. Therefore, our four-bedroom house accommodated three children, two siblings and two sets of parents and other Elders needing an overnight space. Our house outstretched its arms and bulged at the seams. Then about five years into my marriage, my husband became elected Chief of the Band and in this service, I began to learn about politics and Band leadership. I attended meetings with him, gradually learning the administrative practices necessary to operate a Band administration.

The late sixties brought struggles to self-government and self-determination of the political organizations, the Native Brotherhood and the North American Indian Brotherhood. Their charismatic leader, George Manuel, was a key organizer for the local, regional and international Indigenous communities. I began to be politicized, which came at a cost to my family. My husband's struggles with alcohol abuse and our marital discord resulted in our separation after 14 years of marriage and after having three children. I returned to school once again, taking courses that would help the community, such as life skills, to help us 'adapt and assimilate.' Of course I was unaware of the word assimilate back then. My journey through education took on a whole new meaning when I began to realize what happened to us as a people and of course my experience became my bias and point of reference when I attended college courses in the 70's. I would correct my anthropology instructor regarding our tribal practices to the detriment of my marks, thus began my re-socialization in the classroom. I learned to play a little game, wait it out and tell them what they wanted to hear. I later learned in some classes that it was ok to preface my comments with "In my experience" all the while instructors did not really get it. Nor did they often want to.

My life took on a pseudo reality, as others and I worked to govern ourselves, forming Band administrations and area administrations tackling economic development and other concerns, for our distinct society. Other leaders attended university to gain more information and brought these words/ideas home to help the struggle to advance. These struggles continue today. In the 1970's I chose to work in the social service area because I felt we needed healthy soldiers to fight the uphill battle as the evidence of the intolerable acts experienced by our people resulted in many to be drowned in "firewater." This also pointed to developments needed in the education and care of children, thus social work gave me a direction for working with this population. Over the years I have been a self-taught, on-the-ground type of administrator, and leader and it wasn't until the late 1980's that I began a formal quest for college education. During this time I fulfilled the role of a woman in a small reserve community as informal leader, organizer, and volunteer for community functions, fundraising and celebrations.

3.4 Formal Education, Indigenous Studies, and Eldership

In the 80's a felt need for formal training, education, and support for me and other caregivers in our tribes in the Thompson and Shuswap resulted in developing classes for ourselves called *Native Human Services*, where a few women identified what was needed and who we could find to give us education one week per month so that we could continue our work in our home communities which were riddled with despair and hopelessness. We found teachers with Masters of Education degrees and Cultural/Spiritual leaders such as Lee Brown, Phil Lane, Martha Many Grey Horses, Lorraine Brave, David Grant, Bill Mussel, Patrick Paul, Rick Weber, John Lee Kootenkoff, Thomas Kelly and Tony Stickel. All of these teachers were versed in the gifts of spiritual vision and love. It was in this program that I finally got connected to our spiritual ways, which was what I had been seeking all my adult life. I developed my cultural identity and the gifts of spirituality, in addition to the development of other self-dimensions such as the physical, emotional, and mental. These Indigenous Knowledge areas gave me a peace and understanding for which my soul was seeking.

I, and about 300 people in Kamloops, experienced, learned and taught this *Native Human Service Program* and through its creation we developed a two-year program, which ran from 1980-87. The curriculum for this program evolved with us, as leaders and the teachers, who recognized that emotional healing time was required as students learned of the pain caused by our colonization. This program became a healing and learning place for us all. We took the time needed to process the emotional work required. We were fully engaged in our program and learning the things which we needed. Each instructor had a gift that assisted us in our wholistic development and the teachings of the circle (medicine wheel), eagle feather and drum became alive. We recognized that as Indians we had not vanished after all. I am including a portion of Dr. Lee Brown's (2004) dissertation on the *Native Training Institute* where I began my wholistic journey to enlightenment.

I am the creator of my own destiny and I am willing to share with my family, my people and community at large my experiences for reconnection to my people and culture, from which I have been disconnected for too long. What follows next is the verbatim text of my experiences and perspectives that were documented by Dr. Lee Brown as Case Study #4. I believe this text demonstrates an imperative part of my transformation and liberation as a First Nations woman formerly controlled by the Indian Act and subsequent Acts affecting our peoples since contact. This decolonizing process is an act of the reclamation of my heritage, Indigenous knowledge and spirituality. With much deliberation, I have decided to include this excerpt from Dr. Lee Brown's PhD thesis (2004, pp.113-119), with his permission. The next section describes my story of wholistic healing, learning and liberation as an example of the kind of education that is possible when an Indigenous process oriented curriculum is implemented.

3.5 Case Study 4: Marie Anderson

Marie, a member of the Cooks Ferry Indian Band, had a stable childhood filled with strong family values and teachings from her father and mother. She relates the story of how her father, Jacob Anderson, would share teachings:

> We would just sit there and he would talk or tell me stories. He paid a lot of attention to us. He talked to us and he told us things. I think one time I remember we lay on our backs and we were watching clouds and he would say, "Does that look like anything to you?" To this day I still look at the clouds and I see images in the clouds and that is from him. (Interview, January 30, 2003, p. 3)

Marie's father and mother went to great lengths not to send her to residential school. This included boarding her out with relatives so she could attend public school. She states:

> ... the other teaching that I think I really got from him was because mother and father didn't send us to residential school. In that decision they taught us that it was okay to go against the grain, you know, to go against the tide. They discovered alternatives for us and figured out a different way for us to go to school for as long as they could. (Interview, January 30, 2003, p. 3)

Marie became involved with the NTI as an organizer and developer of the program. She was interviewed for this thesis both as a student and as an administrator of the program. Marie had attended a few classes at Cariboo College but had not been excited by the non-Native content and orientation. However, at the NTI she experienced a holistic education that included spiritual/cultural teachings and this created a sense of connection that led her to continue her education and eventually receive a Master's degree in Social Work.

3.5.1 Physical Realm

In the physical realm, Marie defines the essence of a dual process of healing and learning. She comments that she learned both about fasting and nutrition. Fasting, on the physical level represents the letting go of food and the cleansing and purification of the body. Nutrition is the learning that can create better health and develop a sound physical foundation for learning. Here, Marie articulated the twin process of healing the negative and learning the positive in the physical realm. She comments:

> Through the NTI, Native Human Services training program I stopped drinking altogether because I felt that was a detriment. You know, detrimental to my physical body. When you make a life changing decision like that I think you strive also to become fit physically. (Interview, January 30, 2003, p. 11)

3.5.2 Mental Realm

In the mental realm, Marie identifies several areas of resolution. First, she resolved the negative beliefs about being a First Nations person. Second, she resolved the issue around the validity of Aboriginal knowledge and this resolved personal issues with regard to self and its relationship to learning Aboriginal and non-Aboriginal forms of knowledge that developed "clarity... that it was okay to be me" (Interview, January 30, 2003, p. 9).

Marie comments on the time when it was not popular to be a First Nations person. She states that teachings reestablished the pride she had in herself;

> … there was this period in time when it was not really popular to be an Indian or First Nations person. It was a very negative thing. People didn't want to identify with First Nations because there was lots of prejudice. There was lots of Negativity around it. So what it brought back I think was a pride in one's heritage and from that pride one could only gain strength (Interview, January 30, 2003, p. 9).

Marie describes that she was very conflicted with regard to Aboriginal and non-Aboriginal knowledge. She states that "growing up over the years it felt like we were turned, you know we would almost say assimilated; we had turned into non-Native people" (Interview, January 30, 2003, p. 8). This perception created the feeling that it was necessary to give up one's self to become educated. I had internalized the thought; I had to forsake my being, in order to be educated" (p. 12). Marie believed that education based on "white is right learning" could be "cultural suicide" (p. 12). This conflict created a block to learning that was resolved when she realized that both forms of knowledge could be learned and incorporated into a strong Aboriginal self.

> ... Somehow through this process of the NHS Native Training Institute I realized that I could be in both worlds. I could do both and not give up on myself or my Native self and be part of another learning institution. I had the ability to be both. So I feel like that sort of, reservation or reticence to go to a public institution was taken away or evaporated. When I began to learn and maybe it also was because some of the teachers had gone to other institutions and still embraced their traditionalism showing me that I could indeed be the same way. I didn't have to relinquish anything. I could only stand to gain something. (Interview, January 30, 2003, pp. 12-13)

Marie shared a story about riding a double horse that represented the resolution of this conflict for her.

> ... To live in this world you have like two horses that are galloping. One is the mainstream horse and one is your own horse, your traditional horse. You have a leg on each on and you are going and you are going

> fast. You can do it but the thing you need is balance. You need balance on all four areas. You can ride that horse and you can gallop wherever you want because you have the reins to steer to. It is like riding a double horse. (Interview, January 30, 2003, pp. 17-18)

In addition, Marie commented, that becoming a teacher and doer in the cultural realm was an important part of healing in this dual process. Marie refers to this as contextualized learning. Learning was relevant and valid in her context of being. She states:

> So I kind of learned some contextual things. I was able to contextualize some things. (LB: Such as?) Such as we could do our own teaching and we could do our own learning and it was okay to do that. That was a mental realization that we could, that we had what it took to teach ourselves and to teach others. I think that is a pretty major, that was a major awareness for me because, again, having grown up in a society that said you know, white is right. That is a big mental awakening and that made me feel a lot more confident. (Interview, January 30, 2003, p. 12)

3.5.3 Spiritual Realm

Marie states that she was extremely conflicted in the spiritual realm.

> I think that was one of the greatest conflicts in my life as well .... I felt really conflicted about religion because it was religion that got in the way ... In religion I feel there are restrictions, there are certain ways of doing things, ... What happened in the NTI and NHS was that, like I told you, it was like coming home and again it felt like being connected. That is the only thing I can describe. This is how I describe my own spirituality and that I don't even know if that is spirituality but that is how I describe it. It is like a joy of living, a joy for having all the gifts that have come my way, also, a feeling of responsibility for them to try to pass them along. (Interview, January 30, 2003, p. 13)

Marie talks about her conflict about how religion "got in the way" of learning. This is an example of the kind of block to learning that creates the need for a dual process that includes healing in Aboriginal education. This block was removed by the introduction to cultural knowledge and ceremony. One of the ceremonies was the sage ceremony. Marie commented, as did other interviewees, that after her first sage ceremony she cried for weeks. This emotional release reconnected Marie to her spiritual realm and illustrates how the elimination of a learning block can be accomplished through the release of emotional energy. Marie states that this was an incredible "connection of … mind, body and spirit" though emotional release (Interview, January 30, 2003, p. 7). Here again it is evident that the healing of the emotional realm allows the integration of the self during a holistic educational process.

In addition, in the spiritual realm we find a dual process that involved the healing of disconnection from the culture through the re-establishment of strong cultural connections through spirituality, ceremony and knowledge. Marie describes that she felt disconnected from her cultural context.

> Up to then I didn't know what a smudge was. I didn't know what a pipe ceremony was. I didn't know what a sweat was. I remember going to my first sweat and that was really special because I did go in with my mom. (LB: where was that at?) It was at Spence's Bridge, I went in with my mom and it was just an incredible experience. It was a family sweat and

> we learned how to do that and in the learning of that we connected back to our elders. (Interview, January 30, 2003, p. 8)

Through the NTI, Marie gained the "feeling of connectedness and the whole ability to do ceremony" and the learning of cultural history (Interview, January 30, 2003, p. 8).

> It just seem like so, it was such a welcome knowledge because it felt like a certain validity to my own personal being came over me somehow. Again, a sense of security or sacredness or affirmation, it was just wonderful to hear those teachings, it was incredible. It felt like my ears had just been waiting to hear that. It felt like a really special time for me and consequently I remember during that time reading *Black Elk Speaks* and *Lamedeer*. I really took great care in reading those books. I remember buying those books and going to certain places in my area to read those books. I drove in my car, I went by myself and I went to certain places to read them. (Interview, January 30, 2003, p. 25)

In addition, Marie argues that the culture connection is still important in learning situations today.

> I really feel that the connection to culture still is as important today as it ever was. Because really that is who we are and I think that we, you know like I tell people too, we are a great people, we are still here, all the things that have happened to us, we are still here! We are strong our people are strong. (Interview, January 30, 2003, p. 19)

3.5.4 Emotional Realm

Marie states that her emotionality was turned off before she started the NTI by other school experiences. She had been "immobilized" in her ability to learn (Interview, January 30, 2003, p. 15). Her emotions had been turned off through separation from her family and loss of her cultural self (p. 14). She indicates that she was "grieving" for this loss and that this grieving process had created a stress that "hindered me from being all I could be" (p. 14). Here again is a good example of a block to learning, created by hurt, which must resolved and released before learning can be optimal.

> What happened I remember that the first time we burnt sage I cried. I cried and I cried. I remember I was thinking about it then that I hadn't cried in a long time. (LB: sage burned in class?) Yes, wept, an overwhelming feeling of tears came and I just wept and I have no idea what happened. During that time I wept for probably two weeks straight. Not constantly, but I used to drive from Merritt to Kamloops. I remember driving and I would be crying, crying going home and crying coming back. I just cried buckets, it was incredible but after it all was over I was ready to learn (Interview, January 30, 2003, p. 15).

Marie's emotional development at the institute strengthened her values and helped her realize that she had potential and that she "could realize her own potential" (Interview, January 30, 2003, p. 20). An important aspect of this process was the creation of a cultural vocabulary of feeling (Interview, January 30, 2003, p. 30). This enabled Marie to speak of her emotional states, discharge her hurts and create healing possibilities.

3.4.5 Volitional Realm

In the volitional realm, Marie comments that her will was strong from family teachings but that it was also conflicted. After the NTI she felt the conflict was removed and she had the feeling of being whole and complete. She states that the healing of her conflicted will gave her the "permission to really fly" in the realm of learning (Interview, January 30, 2003, p. 17).

Her comment on the resolution of volitional immobility (ambivalence) is interesting. She stated that the ceremonial emotional healing that is the release of the tears and the negative emotions eliminated the block to potentiality that were established in the volitional conflict created by negative emotional experiences around culture and identity (Interview, January 30, 2003, p. 17).

Brown summarizes my wholistic learning in this way:

> The major outcome of the dual process of learning and healing for Marie was the creation of cultural confidence in the learning process in relation to her identity and sense of self. Marie's case articulates the importance of emotional healing in the removal of learning blocks in the physical, mental and spiritual realms. Her description of this understanding, stated above, is precise. The combination of emotional release and cultural teaching developed the sense of belonging, the feeling of connectedness and confidence in relation to Aboriginal people and ancestors necessary for learning to occur. In addition, Marie states that Native History (prophecies) created validity to Aboriginal knowledge (Interview, January 30, 2003, p. 25). She mentions three qualities of Aboriginal knowledge: sacredness, affirmation and security that were important to her ability to learn. (2004, pp. 113-119 with permission)

I believe this last excerpt brings me to a close with my personal story that focused on my childhood, youth, married life, and the beginning of my Elderhood. The latter will be included in Chapters Five and Six.

3.6 Discussion and Summary

To set my personal story and my thesis research in its historical context before colonialism, I need to reiterate that long ago, before the 'white man' arrived, tribal cultures were intact and had highly functional societies. My tribe, the *Nlakapmux,* situated near the current town of Lytton, was no exception. In 1808, upon the arrival of explorer Simon Fraser in the Lower regions of our territory, he found an *Nlakapmux* Nation whose, "sense of who they were was rooted in an *Nlakapmux* landscape, in the *Nlakapmuxcin*, and in a wealth of ideas that had a history of many generations of teaching, thought, and experience. Their identities did not die with the construction of the Canadian Pacific Railroad" (Laforet & York, 1998, p. 8). Therefore, our tribe had vibrant social, educational, political, spiritual and economical practices.

The next part of the discussion section presents colonial processes and their impact. This information provides historical, political, economic, social, and educational contextual background in which to understand the changes that our people experienced.

When the newcomers arrived in our area in the 1800's the foreign practice of Christianity was imposed basically by the Anglican Church of England. Documents state their involvement with First Nations people in Canada since

1698, through the Society for Promoting Christian Knowledge then through the Society for the Propagation of the Gospel in Foreign Parts. This society's first missionaries started work in North America in 1702 and in the West Indies in 1703. Its charter soon expanded to include "evangelization of slaves and Native Americans." By 1710, the Society for the Propagation of the Gospel in Foreign Parts SPG officials stated that "conversion of heathens and infidels ought to be pursued preferably to all others" (Miller, 1943, p.67, p.76).

In Canada, the *Indian Act* passed in 1858 with the goal to assimilate the 'Indian.' To this end, children were removed from their families at the ages of five and six and lodged in Residential Schools that were staffed by priests and nuns or ex-military men. The last Residential School closed in 1970 in our area. These Residential Schools came into being and by 1920 numbered 16 schools in B.C: nine Catholic and seven Protestant. Indigenous scholar, Blair Stonechild points out child labour issues in Residential Schools:

> Although funded by the Government, the administration of the schools was handed to religious denominations, primarily Catholic and Anglican. Totally removed from their parents and communities children were subjected to a regime of inferior education and frequently spent long hours of labour to enable the schools to function within their inadequate budgets (Stonechild, 2006 p. 20).

Residential school curriculum taught religion, agriculture and housekeeping skills for the boys and girls. And, since then, our children have been brainwashed into thinking they were savage, unworthy and would not amount to much. Many still live with these psychological ravages. Indeed the sentiment of the day, I believe, was to eradicate the 'Indian.' These impacts were derived from subsequent policies to the *Indian Act*. In 1869 the *Enfranchisement Act* was passed, a further attempt at assimilation, this Act stated that women marrying non-Indians and anyone without Indian status would cease to be legally Indian and as a result lose their status. In 1871, B.C. joined Confederation and although Indians were still in the majority they were disallowed recognition and the governor of the new province stated "the days are past when your heathen ideas and customs can no longer be tolerated on this land" (Miller, 1943, p.61). During the settlement of the territory all European families were given the opportunity to acquire 160 acres per family and the ability to purchase another 480 acres. Indians were relegated to small reserves, land which no one really wanted. Today, Indian reserve lands are still held in trust for us, because we remain wards of the Crown. Unknown to the public, today, Band members purchase housing on-reserves with Canada Mortgage and Housing Loans, yet they can never own the land beneath their house.

The other destructive Act passed in 1884 was making the Potlatch and Sundance illegal. At this same time another Act was passed, called the *Indian Advancement Act*. Aboriginal Government practice changed from Hereditary Chief to council representation with the white Indian Agent acting as chairman or chief of a Band. A Band was a construct of the Indian Affairs to separate tribal members and the smaller bands were less threatening to the immigrants that were coming to our province seeking gold and new land. From 1900 to 1910 delegations of Indians such as the Nisga'a, Lil'waat and Thompsons made petitions to England to settle the land question by getting recognition of ownership, yet the decision came that we were mere occupants in our traditional territories, which were continually shrinking. First Nations throughout B.C. and other provinces in Canada are still struggling for these land issues today.

This colonial onslaught continues. How do a people survive this genocide? The fact that we are still here speaks to the resilience of our people and also speaks to our ability to adapt and conform; indeed, we change shape to survive. In my tribe we have many stories, leading us to the concept that we can learn from nature to survive. Therefore, it is my theory that we inherently knew how to do this. And in a way we took our lessons from the water and became neutral or like a still lake, taking our essence to the deep to preserve it, all the while shifting outwardly to the expectations of the newcomers who were trying to transform us from hunter gathers to agriculturists. It is my belief that my people have kept their power as they are still embracing their own identities, be it reclamation or revitalization of the *Nlakapmuxcin* language.

I believe our language, *Nlakapmuxcin*, holds much of our secret knowledge and I am doing my part to transmit the language to *Nlakapmux* people who wish to learn it. Lately, it is my nephew, who has just become a practicing lawyer. The language holds many answers about life and living on the landscape of our territories. The place names, the family connections and genealogies are all connected. We are told it was the custom for people before the newcomer to live in harmony with Earth Mother and her generous bounty, which was necessary for our survival. We were taught we had to look after nature. Our people thank the bird, plant and animal spirits for sacrificing their lives to sustain us. We felt a special kinship to nature, almost as if it was human. Let me share a short experience to exemplify how this kinship seems embedded in our families.

Recently when I took my grandson swimming and he noticed the tree roots in the water, he said to me "Grandma, look at the tree's veins." How profound is that? How in tune with creation he was and how inherent our knowledge is. One needs only to survey the landscape now to realize that progress heeds no living thing, take for example the tree, which is taken for telephone poles, housing, and other uses, usually cut down, with little thought to the life of the tree. Similarly, how our waters are being polluted by effluent from our mills as they dump their refuse without care and respect for the fish and salmon. These waters have been polluted beyond use, even in one generation. Industry is not regulated with an eye to conservation but to the profit margin and all living things are at risk. Salmon is the mainstay of our people, yet, it is becoming less and less a resource because of outside influences. I daresay, it will be, all but a memory very soon unless we take drastic steps now.

The circle or the cycle of life as we knew it prior to colonization is almost just a memory, and I shudder to think that the *Gradual Civilization Act* passed in 1857 was to extinguish the tribal people. This Act stated that the Federal Government legislated that Indians had to be assimilated in order to survive, so inducements were made to leave tribal societies. The relationship of all things animate and inanimate is the basis for life itself, and I know that my ancestors and grandfathers and Grandmothers understood the relationship needed for harmony and balance in our world. Most damaging of all is the soul murder of our people.

The spiritual confusion experienced by many tribal peoples has created a multitude of social ills coupled with poverty and despair. However, today, cultural revitalization of our old ways is becoming a potential solution for us to address decolonization factors. Since about the 1980's there have been pockets of enlightenment caused by spiritual teachers and keepers of the flame of life to reach the people and talk to them of how it was long ago. This interaction has been met with welcome changes toward a more self-determining future. Indeed self-determination became the pathway to healing as people realized their separation from their tribe was central to their loss of culture and being in harmony with nature. It appears that the time of 'enlightenment' has arrived as people study and look inward to heal their pain and estrangement from their homeland and extended families. This pathway to learn what is missing and pursue it to become whole once again is the challenge that modern day educators such as I must face and address today.

I began my doctoral course work in 2006 and enjoyed international Indigenous scholars as instructors, which has been self-affirming, healing and hopeful especially for me as an *Nlakapmux* woman. So far, I recognize that for successful education to occur we must have an orientation, relationship and an entry point, however, when I read, *Look to the mountain (*Cajete, 1994*)*; *I* was reminded of the preparation and support that is needed for the educator. The course helped me to start on the pathway to curriculum design but I felt that I needed more content and process. Therefore, I feel like I am still like Miss Louse sweeping the floor, in a story told by Professor Jo-ann Archibald about the process of learning and teaching:

Miss Louse is a story first told by Elder Vi Hilbert and was re-told by Jo-ann Archibald during her course. The meaning that I got from the story is about the teacher who is sweeping the floor for her students but she creates so much dust, she can no longer see the things she needs to see to teach because of all the dust blowing around. This story inspired me to create another story based on our ancient teachings of the vision quest or our search for a power song. The classroom became my sweathouse and a story emerged. I title my story, *Beaver Teachings.* Mrs. Beaver is an industrious builder for our tribe. Mrs. Beaver has put her thinking cap on and is now praying for a vision and a curriculum to teach her children the art of how to live a complete beaver life. I will continue this story in Chapter Seven.

This brief retelling of my memories of Great Grandmothers' stories is the foundation of whom I am becoming, an Elder in my own right. My story began with the introduction of my origins and introduced my family connections. I followed my life cycle chronologically and spoke of my process of conscientization and acquiring formal education in my adult years that helped me understand the impact of colonization on Indigenous people (Freire, 2004). I concluded the chapter with a discussion of historical, political, and educational colonial attempts upon our *Nlakapmux* people. My *Spilahem* (personal story) not only provides a contextual framework of my thesis and the *Nlakapmux* Grandmothers' stories, it brings us into the current day to better understand how an *Nlakapmux* Grandmother passes on her Indigenous knowledge. But first, *Shinkyap*/Coyote wants us to view and experience another story to deepen our appreciation for Grandmothers' persistence and tenacity for holding on to their Indigenous Knowledge despite a new set of challenges that are presented in the next chapter.

Chapter Four: Outsider and Insider Stories about the Nlakapmux

4.1 *Tshama Toohoosh*: In The Eyes of The Other

The first part of the chapter presents the scholarship of early ethnographers such as Franz Boas and James Teit that portray aspects of life about *Nlakapmux* people from the perspectives of the 'other', who are not *Nlakapmux*. The 'other' perspectives during initial European contact viewed *Nlakapmux* people as underdeveloped and in need of saving through an English education. Much of the documentation of our *Nlakapmuxcin* teachings and learnings, which are held in Museums was collected by Teit, who actually lived among the people from 1888-1910. Boas worked from Teit's field notes, which is an issue that will be discussed in the first part of this chapter. The second part highlights the recent scholarship of *Nlakapmux* people about *Nlakapmux* history, culture, and stories. Publications by Darwin Hanna and Mamie Henry (1995), Annie York, Richard Daley, and Chris Arnett (1993), and Shirley Sterling (1992, 1997) are discussed. I conclude the chapter with a discussion that highlights issues such as misrepresentation, authenticity, and inaccurate cultural interpretations that contribute to the phenomenon of double-consciousness.

Works written about *Nlakapmux* people in my home and adjacent territory include a number of historical texts written by early anthropologists. Most notable is James Teit, a Scottish self-educated ethnographer, who worked under the auspices of anthropologists Franz Boas and Edward Sapir. Teit was married to an *Nlakapmux* woman named Lucy Antko. Sapir surveyed the *Thompson, Lillooet, Okanagan, Shuswap* and *Kutenai* peoples in the South, the *Chilcotin* in the central region and the *Tahltan* and *Kaska* in the Northeast. His collection of works outlines the knowledge as members of these tribes conveyed it to him. Teit is considered one of the foremost non-*Nlakapmux* authorities on our people because of his voluminous documentation of early *Speta'kl* and the stories of *Shinkyap*/Coyote, photographs, recorded songs sung by the *Nlakapmux*, and plant names in Latin. Many scholars rely on Teit's prolific ethnographic work in British Columbia, especially his descriptions of the *Speta'kl* as mythology. I present a cursory investigation of his work by me, an insider of the *Nlakapmux*. Franz Boas first met Teit in the summer of 1894, while Boas was employed in field research for the Committee of the British Association for the Advancement of Science for the Study of Northwestern Tribes. Boas' work was overseen in Canada by Horatio Hale, known as "the father of Northwest anthropology." In 1888 Boas recalled in a journal note how he hired Teit:

> I left the train at Spence's Bridge.... [w]hich is a little dump of three or four houses and a hotel near the station...I went to see a man, a Salvation

> Army warrior and big farmer…supposed to know the *Indians* very well. He sent me to another young man who lives three miles up the mountain, who got married to an *Indian*…he knows a great deal about the Tribes. I engaged him right away (Boas, 1888, *Journal Note).*

Teit became fluent in several tribal languages upon his employment with Boas, despite no formal education beyond the age of 16 in Berwick on the Shetland Islands, near Scotland. He already spoke some German, Dutch, French and Spanish. A self taught botanist, Teit also became an entomologist, a photographer of plants and people and anthropologist, receiving first hand training from Indigenous people he encountered and from Boas.

According to the University of Victoria scholar, Wendy Wickwire (1998) in the *Canadian Historical Review*, Teit published 2,200 pages in 43 works and also produced 5,000 pages of unpublished manuscripts material. More than 2,500 pages recorded by Teit focus on the *Thompson Tribe* (*Nlakapmux*). I have reviewed portions of these documents including the references made in them to Coyote stories and their interpretation. Based on my personal experience and the conversations I have had with Tribal Elders over the years, I have concluded these stories were the oral teaching stories that transmited knowledge from generation to generation.

Indeed an example of *Nlakapmux* pedagogy is *Shinkyap*, the Coyote Trickster, a character that links past and present teachings in our oral *Spetak'l*. I found that in fact these stories are related to the origins of the Tribe and to how the Creator sent Coyote to show the *Nlakapmux* how to transform objects or to transform objects or people into land forms to develop a kinshp link to our *tmix* (land). He also gave instructions for the proper and sustainable use of all creation including the care for people within all creation. This collection of work describes the knowledge as it was spoken by the *Nlakapmux* and then recorded in writing by James Teit. These were early days for Teit to collect data on tribes. Teit was just beginning his ethnographic work in a emerging field of study among the Indigenous people in a newly defined British Columbia (1867).

I query the accuracy of the representation and interpretation of the oral stories he documented in English, which is an issue that I return to in the discussion section of this chapter. The issue is how and if an outsider can truly present an accurate translation of the world view of the *Nlakapmux*, based on his foreign background and therefore on his intrinsically different conceptual view of the world. To his credit, Teit stayed among the people, marrying into the Tribe, therefore establishing kinship ties which placed him within the *Nlakapmux* group despite his outsider status.

Today, Teit's early written works are widely available and include: *Traditions of the Thompson River Indian* (1898) and *Mythology of the Thompson Indians* (1912). They include numerous *Nlakapmux* legends. There is also a collection called *The Thompson Indians of British Columbia (1900)*, which contains geographical details and portrays in a systematic and comprehensive manner the life of individuals and families. This work describes the manufacture and the use of different material for houses and household items, clothing, ornaments, food, travel and trade, welfare, games, sign language, birth, marriage and death and other ceremonies, religion and art.

In yet another collection, Teit's *Traditions of the Lillooet Indians of British Columbia* (1912) contains a collection of 38 stories from whom he refers to as the "real" *Lillooet* and 14 stories from the *Lillooet* of the Lakes. In the upper *Thompson Indians* (1916) Teit draws parallels between European folk tales and *Thompson* legends. He also studied and documented Native life and culture in British Columbia in his other books, The *Shuswap* (1909), *Folktales of Salishan and Sahaptin Tribes* (1917) and *The Salishan Tribes of the Western Plateau* (1930).

In 1909 Teit began to assemble a large British Columbia basket collection of information, which he deposited in 1910 and 1911 at the Field Museum of Natural History in Chicago. His basketry notes, sketches, and photos were edited by Boas' students, Herman Karl Haeberlin (who died partway through the project) and Helen Heffron Roberts. Teit's notes indicate that basket-making was a thriving practice until 1928 and then it declined substantially. However, I know that baskets continued to be made for family use to the 1950's.

In his role as 'self-made' but paid researcher, James Teit spent countless hours among our people, learning the language and culture. He submitted hand written material, taped legends and songs, and sent photographs to Boas and the Smithsonian in Washington, DC and in New York. However his work does not credit his *Nlakapmux* informants for their assistance and their knowledge. As I scrutinize Teit's writings in regard to these changes to our lives, I found that he included information about material aspects of culture but he did not speak of the cultural changes or impact of these changes upon the *Nlakapmux* people. At times, I believe that ethnographers made their own changes to the representation of Indigenous people as indicated in the next source of literature.

The book, *A Photographic Collection, the Interior Salish Tribes of British Columbia* by Tepper (1987) from which I have permission to use particular *Nlakapmux* photos, is both useful and questionnable. These photographs are priceless, for not only the historical archive, but for my family collection. However, I wonder about the portraits' settings, which were obviously set up by Teit. As an example, many of the men posing in Teit's photos have suits or other European clothing, suggesting that he not only photographed them but he also provided attire as he thought Nlakapmux should be displayed. In the traditional society of the *Nlakapmux* (British Columbia interior), the choice of apparel and its quality depended on the day's activities, the family's wealth and the maker's skills. The choice of decoration expressed personal messages of artistry, social position and dreams. Whose suits were they in? I remember that my father and Grandfather did not own a suit during their lifetime.

4.2 *Speta'kl*: In Our Songs

James Teit assisted Franz Boas in collecting photos and legend texts, as well as writing descriptions to accompany the songs that were recorded from 1897 to the early 1900's. While the stories on myths and legends may be compromised because they were documented from Western perspectives, recorded songs also have a story to tell. Teit began to collect songs in the Spence's Bridge area in 1897. Both he and Boas used their Edison wax-cylinder machine to record the songs. I listened to the recorded songs, noticing that the notes spoken before each singer describes how singers acted out the stories they were singing after speaking their names. I noticed laughter by the singer immediately after each song.

> An old woman sang the song into the phonograph that serves to 'cleanse' women who had borne twins. She took bundles of fir branches and hit her shoulders and breasts with them while she danced. The song imitates the growl of the grizzly bear because they believe that the children derive from the grizzly bear. An old man sang an old religious song to the sun, a prayer. The gestures were very expressive. He raised his hands up high and looked at the sun. Then he lowered them slowly, pressing them against his chest while he looked down again (Teit, 1900, p.46).

In my assessment, the translation of the songs do not carry their original meanings because the literal translation of the *Nlakapmuxcin* words into English is very difficult because concepts in *Nlakapmuxcin* often do not have English words to portray them. In the song mentioned in the aforementioned quote, my personal *Nlakapmux* knowledge about the songs of the Grizzly Bear were for the protection of the twin children, an important point which is omitted.

Nonetheless, all the songs recorded by Teit were accompanied by numerous and painstakingly written notes. The notes contained complete information including the Native name of the singer, a catalogue number referring to the singer's photograph, the circumstances in which the singer learned or obtained the song, the song-text rendered in the Native language, a rough or word-by-word translation of the text and any other incidental information, such as the age or the importance of the song, or the ceremonial context of the song. As a great many of these songs were from the people of the village, Spence's Bridge, these notes might provide information that may give new insights on that period of *Nlakapmux* history (1897-1910).

In addition to the songs, the musical instruments that were used are now in various museums, including the Royal British Columbia Museum in Victoria, British Columbia, and in the National Museum in Ontario. Another interesting aspect of Teit's work with *Speta'kl* in songs is that more than half of the singers were women: "At a time when most of the collectors were male and collecting only men's songs …concluding that the key musicians in Native communities were the men. Teit recorded more women Nlakapmux singers then men" (Backhouse, 2010, p.58).

Backhouse continues to say, according to Wickwire

> Teit's ethnographies are significant because they are grounded in firsthand experience and offer a sense of depth and sensitivity... they are completely devoid of the standard racist language... For example you will not find terms like 'savage' or 'primitive' or 'lazy' anywhere in his writings (Wickwire cited in Backhouse, 2010, p.59).

In my opinion, despite the focus on women's songs, both Backhouse and Wickwire miss the point that Teit simply did not credit his sources, by acknowledging and naming his *Nlakapmux* informants except in the name of each singer in the songs. I am left wondering whether he did not show gender bias when he recorded more women then men's songs. Or were there more women singers willing to record?

My Great Great Grandfather, Chief *Semxelce'*, was an uncle to *Tetlneetsa; the latter* was supposedly a friend of Teit's. However Teit did not acknowledge his friend *Tetlneetsa's* contributions. It further appears that he collaborated with the *Nlakapmux, Lil'waat* and *Shuswap* Chiefs and, in some instances, he poses with them, however, they are not named. See Figure 4 below as an example where

James Teit (standing in the middle) is shown with *Nlakapmux* Chiefs (Tepper, 1987, p.184).

Figure 4. *Nlakapmux* Chiefs with James Teit

Since Boas was also the employer of James Teit, his biases were undoubtedly present not only in the work done with the *Nlakapmux*. He considered some data to be mere nonsense and therefore he neglected to describe what he chose to discard. Boas' disregard for some aspects of *Nlakapmux* culture makes it impossible for me to accept that he accurately represented our wealth of information made available to him by Teit.

In short, because Boas did not have lived *Nlakapmux* experience he made only academic inferences based on his Western perspective. He also confused the use of the terms *Speta'kl* (ancient stories) and *Spilahem* (a current telling) adding to his interpretative flaws. This has caused me to doubt the accuracy and authenticity of the works produced by Teit and Boas. Based on my cursory analysis of Boas' work, the legends referred to in a book titled *Race, Language and Culture* (1940) must then be reviewed from a *Nlakapmux* speakers' perspective. I, therefore, prefer to obtain oral recollections from the *Nlakapmux* people despite the passage of time and to learn from *Nlakapmux* people who have heard and related to our stories orally and who do not rely on 'outsider' documented stories. *Shinkyap*/Coyote takes us on another learning journey by leaving his tracks for us to follow.

4.3 *Shinkyap Nlakapmux*: Tracks in our Nlakapmux Landscape

More recent writings by *Nlakapmux* scholars and Elders are included in my review of *Nlakapmux* scholarshiip, which will be used to extrapolate ideas. *Nlakapmux* scholars, Darwin Hanna and Mamie Henry, have published a book called *Our Tellings: Interior Salish Stories of the Nlakapmux People* (1995). This work is a collection of *Nlakapmux* stories elicited from present day Elders and are stories familiar to me from childhood. Their book is a compilation of Interior Salish Stories of the *Nlha7ka'pmx* (their spelling) people.

In my view Hanna and Henry's scholarship is a more accurate reflection of our *Speta'kl* and *Spilahem*. I knew most of the people contributing to the documentation of stories which occurred in 1992. However, in reviewing the contributors' taped dates I found it included older interviews documented in 1971 for the British Columbia Indian Language Project, stories previously gathered by Mamie Henry. These were more detailed than those taped in 1992. These are the people taped for Henry's project: Anthony Joe (born 1890), Christine Bobb (1890), Rose Skuki (1880), and Mary Williams (1898). These storytellers were the generation preceding many of those taped in 1992. The short biographies in the book paid honor and respect to the storytellers. Evidently, however, according to Louie Philips, one of the Hanna and Henry storytellers, he knew of people who could tell one story from nightfall to daybreak, but they were now nonexistent. Many of the storytellers in Hanna and Henry's collection had short versions of old Speta'kl.

As a matter of fact my mother Mary Anderson, *Ciceatko* (1909-1999) had been asked to share several stories with the writers, which she did, until she was asked to sign the waiver for ownership. My mother stalled and refused, saying:

> I cannot sign this paper, it says I can no longer own my own story and can never tell it again. Since I have many grandchildren I view it as a loss to my future generations, especially if it precludes me and my family from sharing my stories with them (Mary Anderson, Conversation, 1993).

She disputed the loss of her intellectual property rights. She chose not to allow her stories to be included in the book. The essences of her stories are embedded in me and I can pass them to my descendants. They are in my living memories evidenced by my interpretations for teachings and learnings contained in *Speta'kl* (teaching /storytelling). The issue of property rights, when documenting our stories, has not been defined to date and probably requires more research and decisions made about how this issue will satisfy our *Nlakapmux* people.

Nlekepmux author and Elder Annie York (1993) documented parts of her Indigenous knowledge by working collaboratively with several ethnographers on topics such as *Nlakapmux* botany, and the landscape and the meaning of petroglyphs. These writings are valuable resources to examine, extrapolate and support oral knowledge and transmission methods. *Nlakapmux* ways of transmitting knowledge are examined in York, Daley and Arnett's book, *They Write their Dreams on the Rocks Forever* (1993). Their book is about the petroglyphs and pictographs (art and spirit forms on rocks or rock paintings of the *Nlakapmux*) created by vision questors not so long ago and how they are interpreted by Annie York. These authors contribute to our understanding of Indigenous knowledge through the English language.

Annie York describes, among many other things, the solitary spiritual meditations of young people in the mountains, a form of education once essential to all those who wished to succeed in life with their particular talents. Astrological predictions, herbal medicine, winter spirit dancing, hunting, shamanism, respect for nature, midwifery, birth and death are some of the topics that emerge from Annie's reading of the trail signs and other cultural symbols painted on the rocks.

Stones are the most enduring witnesses and teachers of our *Speta'kl* and *Sphilem.* They are the Grandfathers and Grandmothers who have withstood and survived our own journey of changes. They tell us of the "transformers" who travelled the land when the world was new and accomplished heroic and creative feats. One example among the numerous ones that are to be found throughout our original *Nlakapmux* territory are images of the human feet that can still be seen in the woods near the Stein river. The understanding that the transformers left these traces for us in stone is contained in one of our *Nlakapmux Speta'kl* stories, passed on to us from generation to generation:

> *Sesukii'n* and *Seku'lia* were part of the group of transformers known as the *Shkwitkwatl"* that came from *Shuswap* country and reached Styne Creek (the Stein river) one day at dusk and found a number of people living in an underground lodge just North of the creek where dogs began

> to howl when they approached. There, they transformed a man who made fun of them, his house and the people living there, into stone. Upon leaving, *Sesukli'n* left the mark of his right foot on a stone. A little farther down the river, *Seku'lia* left the mark of his left foot (York, Daley & Arnett, 1993 p.270).

Embedded in this story are the mores for everyday living, to show respect to 0thers, lest some undesirable outcome occurs by not following good life teachings. As reminders of their passing, the *Shkwitkwatl* also changed the "*Speta'kl* people" (pre-human people with animal characteristics and gifted in magic) into real animals and into rocks and boulders with remarkable shapes. Many "legend rocks", as they are referred to by Native Elders, are visible today in the Stein Valley *Nlakapmux* Heritage Park. These are the sentinels of our *timiux* (the land), where our spirit lives.

Another reminder of the mythological age is that certain rock paintings in the valley are said to have been made by the *Shkwitkwatl* and still visible today. The majority of the rock paintings for which the valley is famous, however, were made by our *Nlakapmux* ancestors in special sacred places on our land, which hold for us a special and powerful spiritual meaning and are the source of our spiritual strength.

Nlakapmux scholar Shirley Sterling's book, *My Name is Seepeetza* (1992) and her doctoral dissertion entitled *The Grandmother Stories* (1997) illustrate *Nlakapmux* orality through the written word in English. She introduces the concept of teaching through *Speta'kl* (teaching/storytelling) and informs the reader of her critical praxis. Sterling privileges her *Nlakapmux* voice throughout both works, therefore illustrating a transition from *Nlakapmux* orality to English written words. She qualifies her Grandmothers' life stories as more than survival but a legacy to be embraced, evidenced by her belief that these stories are her gifts to her descendents to help them live successfully.

Shirley Sterling's book, *My Name is Seepeetza* (1992), includes a description of *Speta'kl* as the Coyote teachings and of *Spilahem* as a description of lived experience, which confirms to me as an *Nlakapmux* person, scholar and Grandmother of our teaching stories, the difference in interpretation by *Nlakapmux* who truly understand our culture. Shirley's points directly address learnings and teachings of children, illustrating the disparities between informal (*Nlakapmux*) family teachings and formal school lessons. She pursues lines of traditional cultural pedagogy made by and for *Nlakapmux* as links for a more successful outcome for students. Her description of how environment greatly affects the learning experience for First Nations children cannot be overstated.

The descriptions of how a child thrives in a living environs versus a cold, critical environment is documented fully.

4.4 Discussion and Summary

I realize that a great deal of my informal and formal research during my lifetime has been to identify the missing *Nlakapmuxcin* meanings in the literature written by early Europeans who came to our land. Many of the works on *Nlakapmux* history about the pre-contact and early contact periods are from outsiders. I also realize the difficulties in obtaining authenic *Nlakapmux* stories due to translating their original oral nature told in Nlakapmuxcin to the English language and then portraying the stories within a Western academic discipline. There is certainly a benefit that the traditional stories are recorded so that they are accessible to those interested in learning them. However, I strongly believe that I must privilege *Nlakapmux* voice concerning the documentation and interpretation of *Nlakapmux* scholarship. As shown in the earlier review of scholarship by *Nlakapmux* writers, they portray a more accurate and meaningful historical picture of our *Nlakapmux* ways of life. This discussion and summary section presents issues about historical representation and interpretation of *Nlakapmux* stories and highlights the move to present and share *Nlakapmux* knowledge and stories from insider perspectives.

Teit collected his data during the transition period between amateur and professional anthropology. Teit did a considerable service to the *Nlakapmux* people, as a result of his prolific documentation of our oral history, fauna, foods and songs. However, from my standpoint as a *Nlakapmux* person and a scholar, it is fair to say that although I appreciate the documentation of stories I drew from Teit's documents, he has not contributed anything that I or my Grandmothers did not already know from what was passed on to us through generations of my people. In fact there were many misrepresenations and omissions in the work. For example, Teit paid more attention to the objects the *Nlakapmux* used historically, such as an entire volume, complete with diagrams on how to weave a cedar root basket.

The misrepresentations were in the nature of the interpretive meanings of the oral telling of the *Speta'kl*, dubbing them to be mythology. Other issues include the complete omission of names for the *Nlakapmux* people he documented and the lack of personal biographies; as well as not writing about the effects of the dislocation of the people and their families. To be sure these omissions may be more attributeable to Franz Boas. Oral Indigenous knowledge transmission of the *Nlakapmux* people in pre-colonial times and beyond has been carried out for generations. It is abundantly clear to me that the *Nlakapmux* people had a complete world view and their own genre of stories. In fact, Teit's interpretation of the *Nlakapmux* knowledge that he received orally and his documentation in English of stories, has, in my view, contributed to the phenomenon of skeptisism and disregard for *Nlakapmux* knowledge in general and our stories in particular; all of which exemplify the concept of double-consciousness where our culture and our people are represented through others'/outsiders' worldviews and intepretations and where we and others come to believe in these representations. I will use a part of a story *Lakashstique* or *Origin of Light*, which is an open narrative style of our *Speta'kl* to illustrate the difficulties of interpretation. I have portrayed below, in *Nlakapmuxcin*, a portion of an *Nlakapmux* story written in English by Teit, to also illustrate how difficult it is to translate English into *Nlakapmuxcin*.

Figure 5. "The Origin of Light"

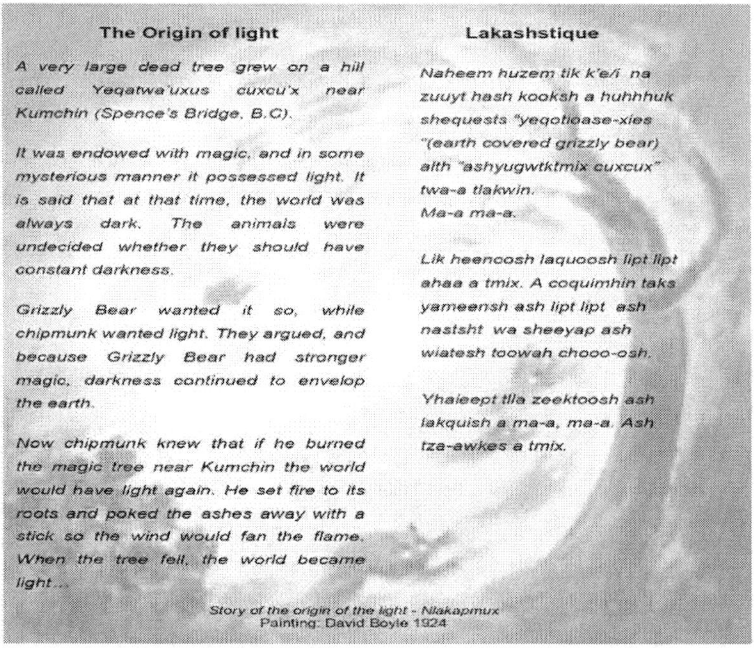

The Origin of light

A very large dead tree grew on a hill called Yeqatwa'uxus cuxcu'x near Kumchin (Spence's Bridge, B.C).

It was endowed with magic, and in some mysterious manner it possessed light. It is said that at that time, the world was always dark. The animals were undecided whether they should have constant darkness.

Grizzly Bear wanted it so, while chipmunk wanted light. They argued, and because Grizzly Bear had stronger magic, darkness continued to envelop the earth.

Now chipmunk knew that if he burned the magic tree near Kumchin the world would have light again. He set fire to its roots and poked the ashes away with a stick so the wind would fan the flame. When the tree fell, the world became light...

Lakashstique

Naheem huzem tik k'e/i na zuuyt hash kooksh a huhhhuk shequests "yeqotioase-xies "(earth covered grizzly bear) alth "ashyugwtktmix cuxcux" twa-a tlakwin.
Ma-a ma-a.

Lik heencosh laquoosh lipt lipt ahaa a tmix. A coquimhin taks yameensh ash lipt lipt ash nastsht wa sheeyap ash wiatesh toowah chooo-osh.

Yhaleept tlla zeektoosh ash lakquish a ma-a, ma-a. Ash tza-awkes a tmix.

Story of the origin of the light - Nlakapmux
Painting: David Boyle 1924

On the right side column, the story is presented in the *Nlakapmuxcin* language. Although it looks shorter, nothing has been omitted. An English word like "endowed" is an interpretive translation of the *Nlakapmuxcin* word/concept, which is impossible to translate. A better translation for 'endowed' would be to use the English phrase 'glowed with light'. Or better yet, to say that this tree was imbued with magical powers; the power to recreate continuous 'light.'

In the English translation, the story does not display the playful tone of the oral story, as there was a contest between Grizzly Bear and the Chipmunk to determine the division between daylight and dark. As an aside, one meaning that I take from the story is that Grizzly Bear could represent English domination of our society through colonizing practices while the Chipmunk is the *Nlakapmux* Grandmother who uses her Indigenous knowledge/stories (the stick) to create a better life (world of light) for her descendants. Another meaning may be, size does not mean strength or having more wisdom. Unless one has lived with traditional story pedagogy of meaning making, the type of understanding that I just shared is missed; then the story is not valued for its epistemological quality.

I have called on my language skills in both *Nlakapmuxcin* my mother tongue and English to scrutinize the literature for authenticity in representation, interpretation and meanings. In my critique, the labeling, categorization, and documentation of *Nlakapmux* myths and legends by Boas and Teit are questionable, especially because it was done by non-*Nlakapmux* people and at the turn of the century. The translation of stories from the oral *Nlakapmuxcin* language into the written English language is flawed. Boas and Teit use words that are simply not used in our culture. The oral refinement in *Nlakapmux* storytelling is determined by the age of the listener. For example, the *Nli'kisentem* story is simply referred to as a Coyote tale. According to my Grandmothers' stories and how it was related to me and other girls, it actually had great teaching and learning lessons about rape and how young girls must be aware of this potential and protect one and each other from unwarranted advances of men. Similarly, the story of *Tapped His Legs* was another warning story for young girls about the unwarranted advances of men.

I take issue with Boas' categorization of our *Speta'kl* and *Spilahem* because they are in the eyes of the other who have not had meaningful learning with the *Nlakapmux*. The categories chosen by Boas comprise 52 stories under the heading *Myths and Tales of the Utamqt* and are further divided into Coyote tales, transformer tales, origin myths, animal tales, hero tales, ancestor tales from Spuzzum, semi-historical tales, tales adopted from the Coast tribes and tales based on European folklore. He collected another 115 tales from the Nicola Valley and Fraser River.

Boas was not educated in the ways of our people. By merely classifying all Thompson stories as mythology in fictional literature Teit and Boas placed them outside the realm of teaching stories. Indigenous scholars the world over are contesting outsider interpretations of Indigenous stories that have not had meaningful involvement or control of the representations by Indigenous people. They are also supported by enlightened mainstream modern-day socio-scientists. Perhaps the definition of "amateur" in the debate about reliable scientific professionalism could be applied to some of the early ethnographers. This definition highlights how I personally place the work of Boas regarding our *Nlakapmuxcin* knowledge.

In contrast, I believe that the strengths of 'insiders' presenting and sharing *Nlakapmux* knowledge and stories to be more authentically represented, especially when the older generation of *Nlakapmuxcin* speakers are intimately involved with representing their knowledge. In my experience there are remaining oral knowledge keepers who have inherent knowledge about the teaching/learning meanings of the stories. The stories written by Boas are not merely tales of mythology and other so called folklore. It appears that the term 'tales' was the common English word for any oral story in the late 1800's. They were also referred to as anecdotes, meaning no weight was conveyed by them because they were not scientifically sound. This was the time period when Boas' work was being completed. The revival of the *Nlakapmuxcin* language may be one way to address the limited representation and interpretation of stories. However, the challenges are great. There are few language speakers remaining among the *Nlakapmux*. The time, interest and resources are also limited. Perhaps new more enlightened *Nlakapmux* scholars of any profession, education, anthropology, sociology and language studies may chose this topic for their contributions. The wholistic dimension of these related disciplines could complement the works in this way to be expedient.

Many present day Indigenous scholars and researchers, especially women researchers like me, "have found that our own personal narratives provide insights into culture and society not afforded by conventional anthropological methods" (Howard-Bobiwash, 1999, p.118). Martine Reid and Daisy Sewid-Smith in their portrayal of Agnes Alfred (1890-1992), *Qwiqwasutinux* Noblewoman, in their book, *Paddling to Where I Stand* advocate that, if First Nations (especially those who are literate), are going to be portrayed in the anthropological literature, then Indigenous people should be the ones doing and being in control of their portrayal/representation, thereby, confronting and changing the negative impact of double-consciousness from scholarship that viewed us from the 'eyes' of the other and that portrayed us as 'the other' (Martine & Sewid Smith, 2004). Therefore, I am including my point of view in the portrayal of the *Nlakapmux* perspective throughout my thesis. I am exercising my *Nlakapmux* right to express myself in this vernacular expressing Nlakapmux scholarship in double-voice and double-consciousness.

Nlakampux perspectives are examined through my *Spilahem* (current personal narrative) but I include stories and teachings that were passed on to me throughout my life by my Grandmothers' *Speta'kl* and *Spilahem*. In the next chapter, my current personal narrative and those shared by the Grandmother voices of my interviewees brings into 'light' the *Spilahem* (teaching) stories, we were familiar with as children.

Chapter Five: *NLAKAPMUX* Grandmother Voices

5.1 Introduction

This chapter presents the *Nlakapmux* Grandmother participants' voices and perspectives in relation to *Shinkyap shau'a'tem* - these thesis research questions:

- How did your Grandmothers pass on *Nlakapmux* knowledge (values, beliefs, and teachings) and pedagogy?
- What were important teachings and pedagogies?
- How did *Nlakapmux* intergenerational learning, oral tradition, and teachings contribute to living a good life?

In following respectful protocol, the Grandmother participants are introduced first with information about their *Nlakapmux* name, birth year and demise where applicable, their family size, number of children and education that they have acquired. The first four participants are community members. The other seven are family members (see Figure 6). I then explain my use of the Medicine Wheel framework for presenting the wholistic analysis that I completed. The Medicine Wheel, although not perfect, works well for portraying the wholistic nature of *Nlakapmux* learning.

I turned to a traditional form of *Nlakapmux* women's work to refine the analysis and to portray the Grandmothers' remembrances and perspectives. Both the Medicine Wheel and Cedar Root Basket making provide the analytical structure to present the Grandmothers' individual and collective voices. I close this chapter with a summary of the Grandmother *Nlakapmux* concepts and how they are described in the Cedar Root Basket metaphor as the foundational principles that are illustrated in the next chapter.

5.2 Introducing the Grandmother Participants

Each Grandmother's introduction is in her voice. She indicates her birth date, birth place, and that of her family including parents, Grandmothers, and Great Grandmothers. Because my study focuses on Grandmothers, not all Grandfathers are identified. Each Grandmother was asked to share her "biggest teaching." These teachings are ones that they have strived to practice throughout their lives.

5.2.1 May Voght (Moses)

I was born in 1922 in the Nicola Valley. I did not attend Residential School. My Grandmother was Old Edith, she is the one who took care of me and taught me many things before I was nine years old. I was forced into marriage to a man when I was just 16 years old and had a son with him. I later got together with my late husband, Fred Voght, who was my companion for over 50 years. We had eight kids and who have uncounted children who I helped raise over the years and am sad to say, three of my sons have already died (May V).

5.2.2 Patsy McKay (Philips)

I was born in 1936 in Speentlem Flats near Lytton to the Philips family. My Grandmother taught me many things before I went to Residential School for eight years. My fondest memories are about the home I enjoyed with pets and generosity of our family providing for visitors on their way to the Stein. The biggest lesson I learned was to do 'no harm' (Patsy M).

5.2.3 Jean York (Albert), Laxpetko

I was born in Merritt in 1942 to Theresa (1912) and Wilson Albert, Grandmother Lucy Albert (1883) and great-Grandmother Laxpetko, Catherine Albert. I was sent to Residential School for 10 years. I have one daughter and two sons and one grand-daughter and two grandsons. The biggest lesson I learned from my Grandmother was that I must go to school to learn the Whiteman's ways and become competitive in the modern world (Jean Y).

5.2.4 Leona Lafferty

I was born in Merritt 1965 to Dorothy Sam (1930 – 1969), Grandparents Dennis and Louisa Sam, Grandparents Tim and Lily Shuter (Bent) on mother's side. My Grandmother was Victoria Dumont. My Grandmother teachings came through Louisa Sam, birth year 1910. Louisa had seven children. I have four children and two grandchildren. I did not attend Residential School. My biggest teachings were to revere family and the importance of living in the natural world when possible, harvesting nature and growing own food (Leona L). Below is a photograph taken during one of our family gatherings.

Figure 6. Anderson Family August 2001

(Percy, Judy, Lorna, David, Trudine, Mary (Mother), Marie, Bernice, Aiona, and Grace)

5.3 *Nlakapmux* Sibling Biographies

5.3.1 Lorna Sterling (Anderson), *Chinmalx*

I was born in Ashcroft in 1942 to Mary (1909) and Jacob (1911) Anderson, maternal Grandmother Whatpalx Clara Edmonds Philips (1868 – 1949), great-Grandmothers *Tiila* Beatrice Anderson (1870 – 1958), who was born in *Inkukuk/peykyst* Reserve and Alice Yamelst, who was from the Cornwall reserve (1880 – 1964). My paternal great-Grandmother *Lamiinak* Jane Drynock was from the *Inkukuk/peykyst* reserve (1870 – 1952). I did not attend

Residential School. I have five children, all finished grade 12 and two have Masters in Education, one daughter has a PhD in Psychology, one daughter in Alcohol Certificate Counselling and a son is in computer programming. My biggest teaching was to take care of family throughout the life span (Lorna S).

5.3.2 Trudine Dunstan (Anderson)

I was born in 1945 to Mary (1909) and Jacob (1911) Anderson, maternal Grandmother *Whatpalx* Clara Edmonds Philips (1868 – 1949), great-Grandmothers *Tiila* Beatrice Anderson (1870 – 1958) who was born in *Inkukuk/peykyst* reserve and Alice Yamelst who was from the Cornwall reserve (1880 – 1964). My paternal great-Grandmother *Lamiinak,* Jane Drynock, was from the *Inkukuk/peykst* reserve (1870 – 1952). I attended Residential School from grade six to ten. My twin girls have Masters in Education and Bachelor of Social work and my son is now my caregiver. My biggest lessons learned are self-sufficiency, hard work, embracing our Nlakapmux names and living an extended family concept (Trudine A).

5.3.3 Judy Blades (Anderson), *Lamiinak*

I was born in 1946 to Mary (1909) and Jacob (1911) Anderson, maternal Grandmother *Whatpalx* Clara Edmonds Philips (1868 – 1949), great-Grandmothers *Tiila* Beatrice Anderson (1870 – 1958), who was born in *Inkukuk/peykyst* reserve and Alice Yamelst, who was from the Cornwall reserve

(1880 – 1964). My paternal great-Grandmother *Lamiinak* Jane Drynock, was from the *Inkukuk/peykyst* reserve (1870 – 1952). I attended Residential School from grades four to ten. I have four children and six grandchildren. My four children are all self-sufficient and my biggest teachings are to keep the *Nlakapmux* traditions alive by growing an organic farm (Judy B).

5.3.4 Aiona Carmelita (Anderson)

I was born in 1952 to Mary (1909) and Jacob (1911), maternal Grandmother *Whatpalx* Clara Edmonds Philips (1868 – 1949), great-Grandmothers *Tiila* Beatrice Anderson (1870 – 1958), who was born in *Inkukuk/peymanoos* reserve and Alice Yamelst, who was from the Cornwall reserve (1890 – 1964). My paternal great-Grandmother *Lamiinak* Jane Drynock, was from the *Inkukuk/peymanoos* reserve (1870 – 1952). I attended Residential School from grade two to nine. I have three children: one son is a lawyer and one son has a Bachelor of Fine Arts and my daughter is a hairdresser and she has two sons. My biggest learning/teaching is carrying on the *Nlakapmux* teachings to the community through counselling and Fine Arts (Aiona A).

5.3.5 Bernice Anderson, *Whatpalx*

I was born in 1953 to Mary (1909) and Jacob (1911) Anderson, maternal Grandmother *Wharpalx* Clara Edmonds Philips (1868 – 1949), great-Grandmothers *Tiila* Beatrice Anderson (1870 – 1958) who was born in

Inkukuk/peykyst reserve and Alice Yamelst, who was from the Cornwall reserve (1880 – 1964). My paternal great-Grandmother *Lamiinak* Jane Drynock was from the *Inkukuk/peykyst* reserve (1870 – 1952). I attended Residential School from age five to twelve, and acquired grade eight. I have two sons, one has a Masters in English and three children; the other is a skilled roofer. My biggest teaching is to be hard working and providing assistance to anyone in need (Bernice A).

5.3.6 Verna Billy-Minnabarriet

I was born in Ashcroft to Percy (1927 – 2001) and Maria (Pierro) (1933 – 2003) Minnabarriet. My paternal great-Grandmother was Nancy Minnabarriet (1866 – 1970), my Grandmother was Mary Anderson (1909 – 2009), my adopted Grandmother is May Voght Moses (1926), and my maternal Grandmother was Rose (Burke) Pierro (1898-1969). I did not attend Residential School. I acquired a Bachelors degree in Commerce (UBC), a Masters in Education and Masters Arts and Community Economic Development (SFU), and will soon complete an Education Leadership Doctorate at UBC. I have one son (Kristopher Tyler Billy) who has a Bachelor of General Arts and Community Economic Development (SFU) and he has a baby son (Rocket Tyler Sinclair Billy). I have a daughter (Heidi Suzzanne Billy) who has a Diploma in Community Economic Development, Film Making and she is a certified

Industrial First Aid Paramedic. My biggest teaching is passing on unconditional help to all who ask it (Verna BM).

5.3.7 Yvonne Shuter, *Shepeenak*

I was born in Merritt on June 4, 1961 to Marie and Wainwright Shuter (1937-2001), maternal Grandmother Mary Anderson (1909 – 2009), paternal great-Grandmother Rosie Boston (1880 – 1961), and paternal Grandmother Christine Harry (1915 – 1950). I have two brothers, Mitchell and Colin. I did not attend Residential School. I acquired a Bachelors degree in Social Work (2000). I have one daughter, Alexis McPhee, who has one son,Nathan Silvey and my son Jeremy.Jeremy has one daughter named Alsea. My biggest teaching is to be productive, hardworking and live the traditions (Yvonne S).

Each Grandmother is honoured for her remembrances that focus on learning relationships and experiences with her Grandmothers in a number of ways. First, samples of each Grandmother's remembrances are shown in a wholistic overview using the physical, spiritual, emotional and mental realms, which is another way of getting to know each Grandmother (see Table 1). Second, a wholistic oriented discussion of the Grandmothers' perspectives follows the chart presentation.

5.4 Medicine Wheel: Wholistic Analysis

In a description of the Medicine Wheel (Lane, Bopp, Bopp, & Brown, 1985), one's life journey often begins in the East with the birth of the child, then the journey continues in the remaining three cardinal directions represented by the life phases of youth, adult and Elder. There are teachings specific to each phase, which are not necessarily completed before moving on to the next life phase. In the book *The Sacred Tree,* the authors discuss the various meanings of 'four' in relation to the Medicine Wheel directions:

> There are four dimensions of "true learning." These four aspects of every person's nature are reflected in the four cardinal points of the medicine wheel. These four aspects of our being are developed through the use of our volition or will. It cannot be said that a person has totally learned in a whole and balanced manner unless all four dimensions of her being have been involved in the process (Lane, Bopp, Bopp, Brown, 1985, p.29).

Of significance too, is to remember on one's life journey the wheel has many gifts for each direction and it has always been our challenge to continue to learn and persevere in passing on our lessons of the four directions to the younger generations.

In my *Nlakapmux* ways of knowing I illustrate my Grandmother perspectives in the four Medicine Wheel realms where the spiritual is in an opposite direction to the physical, and the emotional is in the opposite direction to the mental realm (see Figure 6). I understand that there is tension between the physical and spiritual realms. When we are born we are in the physical realm and as we age we develop spiritually, and eventually become the wise Elder. When we are young/youth we are in the emotional realm and move along or mature into the mental realm.

I used the concept of the Medicine Wheel's four realms of physical, spiritual, emotional, and mental to illustrate the Grandmothers' perspectives about *Nlakapmux* pedagogy and ways of passing on traditional values, beliefs, and teachings. I recognize that the Grandmothers' examples of pedagogy may fit one or more realms, but for the purposes of demonstrating their meaning and relationship to a wholistic form (Medicine Wheel) of knowing, I placed them in one realm. I presented this wholistic analysis framework to the Grandmother participants. They were excited about this form of analysis and gave their approval for me to present it in this thesis in various formats, such as in Table 1 below.

Table 1. *Nlakapmux* Grandmothers' Wholistic Chart

RESPONDENT GRANDMOTHER	PHYSICAL REALM	SPIRITUAL REALM	EMOTIONAL REALM	MENTAL REALM
Aiona A.	Help with the chores, dishes and sweeping, berry picking	Children were shown kindness, did not scold them, protected from physical and emotional injury such as name calling	Children never left behind Share with others kids	When fell into a cactus patch granny picked each prickle out of my hand ever so gently; learning to be gentle with others
Trudine D.	Made tools with natural things, bone awls, buckskin from deer hides, dyes from plants, necklaces from seeds, preparing for baby, making cradleboards from birch bark, gloves and	Each season had celebration ceremonies. All creation had a value and we are to protect it by using everything usable, wasting nothing of food or/of creation. Asking prayers for rain for the garden.	Care for self and listen to one another. All stories had a built in lesson shown by Bigfoot, Bobcat, Crow, Coyote and Loon. Grew bonding by saying prayers with Grandmother daily. Sharing talks and stories with	Taught us to teach the younger children by storytelling and creative play and listening to the morals of a story Taught us memory and listening skills, Storytelling with a moral attached for the central character taught consequence through repetition,

RESPONDENT GRANDMOTHER	PHYSICAL REALM	SPIRITUAL REALM	EMOTIONAL REALM	MENTAL REALM
	moccasins from deer hides, baskets from pine needles, bear grass and cedar root Cleanse sweating with Grandmother in early morning Being present for life events	Asking for strength to work in the garden till age 90's	Grandmothers into their 90's.	interspersed with humor. I learned a lot of things from her but one thing I do remember I guess you could call cultural knowledge is she taught us how to make the baskets you know [from] the cedar roots. I remember we all started making one and I think I probably got a piece maybe this big (six inches in diameter)….I never finished it but I remember working on it. And I do remember how hard it was to try to make it really even. Hers was so immaculate I remember it

RESPONDENT GRANDMOTHER	PHYSICAL REALM	SPIRITUAL REALM	EMOTIONAL REALM	MENTAL REALM
				being so neat. And of course I was really young. I don't know how old I was. But I do remember her teaching us how to do that cedar root basket. (Nlakapmux) goohoom Taught we had relationship with the Great Spirit early from before birth, continually told stories of prayers for us as children and then for our continued safety. Storytelling to us and others was possible well into age 90's demonstrated by Grandmother

RESPONDEN T GRANDMOT HER	PHYSIC AL REALM	SPIRITUA L REALM	EMOTION AL REALM	MENTAL REALM
Jean Y.	Shown how to keep our physical being and clothes clean	Singing humorous songs to create a happy atmosphere, telling jokes for laughter.	Sharing our Shinkyap stories with each other when needed	Taught sharing humorous stories to others or in a group in order to laugh together Urged to get a education to have freedom of choice
Bernice A.	Taken to school	Celebrating life transitions	Family or group sharing was fun	Life Lessons had a purpose or goal and was appropriate at all stages of development
Verna BM	Cleanse sweating with Grandmot her early in the morning Picking fruit and produce with Grandmot her	Prayers were said at meals and at night and before traveling Prayer sweating with Grandmothe r, prayer for rain for the crops	Had little children's protectors in the cradles. A new cradle was made for each baby and the cradles were kept with care. Saying prayers with Grandmothe	Prayers were said to communicate with the great spirit and to ask for blessings, guidance and protection. Develop imaginations by visualizing pictures in clouds, in the landscape

RESPONDENT GRANDMOTHER	PHYSICAL REALM	SPIRITUAL REALM	EMOTIONAL REALM	MENTAL REALM
			r daily	Taught we had a relationship with the Great Spirit Showed me how to trade for goods with food from the garden and orchard Taught the Grandmothers to be strong, rode horses till their 90's
Lorna S.	Demonstrated the task to be replicated when child asked	Never hit, punished nor scolded	Demonstrated the task by storytelling and repetition	Demonstrated a task over and over again
Yvonne S.	Told lessons in age appropriate stories- all in the Nlakapmux language. Told	Speaking to the departed spirit at funerals was a custom. Telling the spirit they were not of this world now but	Helpful to Grandmothers by being quiet and behaving at these hard times and when grandmother asked for help, to give	Taught to be quiet, respectful of the funeral, wake and burial customs. Taught death was a transition to the spirit world,

RESPONDEN T GRANDMOT HER	PHYSIC AL REALM	SPIRITUA L REALM	EMOTION AL REALM	MENTAL REALM
	about easy birthing by walking uphill, dropping pebbles and chanting make my baby birth easily just as this stone falls from my fingers Small Children protected from the departed spirits by being kept away from bigger gatherings Feeding the baby with breast milk and introducin g plain	were of the afterlife and assuring them we would meet again in the future when we were finished with this earthly life. Pray to be industrious, help elders, parents and take good care of self. Granny would ask us children to retell the story occasionally, (so we learned by repeating it) and she never tired of hearing or repeating the same story. I was proud to be asked to repeat the	it Birthing details given to pregnant girls to show how to help women during childbirth, cutting the cord, cleaning the baby, welcoming the baby. Caring and feeding the baby, allowing the child to cry for exercise and vocal development Sharing with Grandmothe r through the stages of childhood, puberty and adulthood creating bonding with Grandmothe	however, we could commune with our departed ones for advice or support Taught as the eldest child I was keeper of family histories, Taught kinship lines, teaching stories, and stories with entertainment value. Learned dream analysis by sharing dreams. Learning gender roles through Bear stories. Taught to sweat with only my gender or just my family Passed down life phase teachings, babies, puberty,

RESPONDEN T GRANDMOT HER	PHYSIC AL REALM	SPIRITUA L REALM	EMOTION AL REALM	MENTAL REALM
	foods free from sugar. Taking the baby into the forest as a baby to hear the forest sounds Going camping and berry picking as a baby on grandma's back	story and be praised for my ability to do so. Sometimes repeated story night after night. Praying for my baby to be healthy and strong, and have a good life. OK to cry when someone died but kids were not allowed to go to funerals	r in many activities, work and play. Playing with siblings and neighbours before school as families and friends visited often.	parenthood, bartering. Taught the spirit world was a natural progression of life and a transition all must go through Taught by repetition in all storytelling of Indigenous knowledge.
May V.	Went berry picking, food gathering and fishing and hunting on cyclical basis	We went food gathering, hunting and thanking ceremonies, Singing celebratory songs	Songs of thanksgiving were sung during food gathering together and when travelling to and from communities .	Taught the cycle of the seasons for food gathering and preserving food Taught to look after extended family

RESPONDENT GRANDMOTHER	PHYSICAL REALM	SPIRITUAL REALM	EMOTIONAL REALM	MENTAL REALM
Judy B.	Planting gardens, orchards and fruit in the spring.	Growing more food than needed so to share with others by inviting others at harvest time	Told stories by repetition when travelling, working and visiting each other	Taught the seasons to plant, care for and harvest foods.
Leona L.	Planting gardens, orchards and fruit in the spring	Catching more fish than needed so to share with neighbours.	Sharing garden produce with others is rewarding	Taught the seasons to plant, care for and harvest foods and to share with elders by volunteering
Patsy M	Visited relatives often as a family.	Pray and be industrious, help Elders, parents and take good care of self.	The garden planted with care thrives and gives feeling of satisfaction and well being	Taught eldest children were keepers of family histories, traditions and stories Taught shared cultural knowledge zoomt, (puberty) and other age appropriate ceremonies throughout life

During the discussions with the Grandmothers and my subsequent reflections, the idea of cedar root basket making as an Nlakapmux metaphor for making meaning of their stories and experiences emerged.

5.5 Cedar Root Basket Making: *Nlakapmux* Grandmothers' Knowledge

I chose to use *Nlakapmux* basket making as a metaphor to articulate and embody the ancestral knowledge of the *Nlakapmux* grandmothers that I interviewed. Storytelling was the major method of transferring Indigenous knowledge in our oral culture. The way the Grandmother stories unfolded was like the process of weaving a basket. There were times when the stories veered off into other areas seeming not to address the topics being discussed, but through the analysis process their individual and collective ideas illustrate a pattern, value, understanding, or teaching. Each Grandmother stressed the importance of transferring and practicing *Nlakapmux* knowledge so that it was retained by their family member(s).

Cedar Root Baskets and the process of making them were essential to life in pre-contact times. Basketry is the embodiment of the quality of life for the family and community because the baskets provided for all aspects of personal sustenance and well-being. *Nlakapmux* people stored food or water in cedar root and other baskets, used them as cooking vessels, and carried babies in them, which enabled people to travel and visit other territories, connecting them to extended family and allies. The extended family fulfilled individual and collective physical, emotional, mental and spiritual needs as necessary.

In the beginning phase of weaving a basket, the materials are gathered and prepared, then a decision is made about the type of basket to be made. Embedded in this decision are the basket's purpose or function, and its shape and design. In some instances the basket may be a gift or heirloom requiring special thought about the basket's function. A child was always thought of as a gift from the Creator and consistently treated as a gift. Basket making is the perfect analogy to describe the value attributed to the spiritual and practical nature of the child.

The traditional development of the child's whole being was carefully planned and developed from birth onward. Similarly, the knowledge of resources and perseverance of the weaver to complete a cedar root basket, coil by coil, is very much like preparing (teaching) a child to live a good life through weaving together Nlakapmux wholistic teachings. Weaving a cedar root basket involves many scientific methods such as mathematics, visual arts, chemistry, and environmental management. In addition there are spiritual and social protocols to follow. This description fits the interdisciplinary needs to complete the cedar root basket and enables the *Nlakapmux* people to thrive in their environment.

The Grandmothers imparted important societal norms that governed behavior, teachings, practices and love to the younger generations. Grandmothers were the essence of knowledge transmission occurring in any family. Some of the Grandmother participants shared remembrances of learning to make baskets from their grandmothers. They revealed that their grandmothers had high expectations and demonstrated love towards their grandchildren's efforts.

> Of course we lived with Tiilaa our grandmother, well we called her *Ya-ya (Nlakapmux*) and well I learned a lot of things from her, but one thing I do remember I guess you could call cultural knowledge is she taught us how to do the baskets you know the cedar roots. I remember we all started making one and I think I probably [made] a piece [of a basket] maybe this big….I never finished it, but I remember working on it. And I do remember how hard it was to try to make it, really. Hers was so immaculate. I remember it being so neat. And of course I was really young. I don't know how old I was. But I do remember her teaching us how to do that cedar root basket (*Nlakapmux*) *goohoom* (Trudine Dunstan Personal Interview, 2010, p.2).

I use basketry (as a process) to illustrate lessons taught for all realms of the whole being. The physical realm in this process is interconnected to collecting the natural materials to build the basket and growing foods to live in a healthy manner. In the spiritual realm the role of ceremonies to mark important phases of life and achievements such as making one's first basket are discussed. The emotional realm shows the ways of acquiring discipline and perseverance to complete tasks such as basket making and preparing for one's future life roles. In the mental realm, interdisciplinary knowledge, planning, and problem solving are linked to storytelling as one key means to learn various knowledge. This is the complete wholistic basket that holds all the teachings, stories, mores and social customs of the *Nlakapmux* family and community.

5.5.1 Physical Realm

There are many processes to consider when gathering the material for the basket such as protocol, season, timing, who gathers, place, preparation and which Grandmother is going to lead the group. Through years of experience, the knowledge transmission process was so well known that very little explicit direction was discussed among the Grandmothers. A similar pedagogic practice was followed for storytelling: no direction was given; it was left open to interpretation by the listener. We, as young people, were not told explicitly to wake up and then head out to gather.

There were stories of how one gathers, the best place to go, what place was utilized the year before. A story was told about the geography of a place in our natural landscape, but the exact location of cedar trees for making baskets were not identified in order to protect and conserve them. This special relationship to nature's resources resulted in life sustaining plant and, later, gardening knowledge. The Grandmother interviews yielded a number of land-based practices that clearly lead to being strong and healthy physically:

> Granny taught me to walk and run to the garden to pick the vegetables fresh for dinner, how to boil them in little water and eat a variety at mealtimes. She elaborated by saying she had suggested they ride horses to the garden but Granny said it was also important to walk and run. And she taught me the land usage of how to plant, care for and conserve our plants, to eat together (Lorna Sterling, Personal Interview, 2009, p.2).

Another grandmother described her similar experiences:

> And through the seasons to do everything from spring, summer, fall and winter, we food and medicine plant gathered together with the children. In the spring we go dig up all types of edible plants and that's the most things I remember her telling me, the plants are calling us because they are ready to be harvested. You know going for onions (*tatoon*) and potatoes and celery (*hakuu*). Going for picking berries was a welcome activity with grandma. (*Shhqueet*). Everything. But I can't remember, I wish I would've remembered this one root, she'd used to always gather down by Nicola Lake and it was a white root. I've never seen anybody gathering it now but she said it was one of the most important roots of our people because it fight all the diseases and she stressed, physical fitness and developing strength as children to us every day (Leona Lafferty, Personal Interview, 2009, p.1).

Grandmother Aiona Anderson mused:

> But I guess what really impressed me is that I also remember her coming to visit us when she was quite elderly, quite old. And she would ride the horse and she would get off, then I think we would hold the horse and she [would] get off, stepping on the block of wood and I was always amazed

> that she could do that, as an old lady (Aiona Anderson, Personal Interview, 2009, p.1).

The value of good health is clear from all the Grandmother stories. All families and Grandmothers had huge gardens and orchards in our growing years, which was the Grandmother's domain. She was hardworking, methodical, and enduring. She worked according to the weather and growing cycles. The entire family and the community benefited from her hard work and her produce.

> Grandmother taught me, Old T*iilaa* taught me some things about drying food. How to peel an apple for drying, cut it in half and cut it half this way, then cut it half again, quarter it up and I can still dry the apples, remember, we had about ten apple trees (Lorna Sterling, Personal Interview, 2009, p.1).

Another grandmother remembered the raspberry field as Grandmother's treasure,

> I have raspberry canes from her field, she had shared these with my mother-in-law in Lytton and then I got them from her to plant in my Kamloops garden (Trudine Dunstan, Personal Interview, 2010, p.2).

In keeping with the extended family teaching of giving back and the *Nlakapmux* Grandmother tradition today, she invites family and friends to harvest in July when raspberries are prolific and ready to pick. Another speaks of her organic farming endeavors on the old homestead. She talks enthusiastically about her organic gardening:

> I remember the garden and the orchards and fields thriving and I want my grandchildren to experience that. That is one of the reasons I am gardening organically on the old homestead today (Judy Blades, Personal Interview, 2010, p.1).

The Grandmother participants had many memories of activities pertaining to physical exercise and eating healthy wholesome vegetables and fruits, all grown by their Grandmothers. These Grandmothers also wished to pass this food knowledge and value of healthy living to their grandchildren. "The activities learned as a child stick with you," as one Grandmother said. The development of the physical self included gardening, cooking, preserving and exercising. These activities are very much a part of Indigenous knowledge, although the *Nlakapmux* are in transition today concerning place based/environment knowledge. Grandmothers still pass down their plant and gardening knowledge for their families and communities' preservation.

> By growing the garden, by making that raspberry patch, which was her treasure [where] she worked it every year pruning it, mulching it and doing all kinds of things, that was what she did and she used to do big things with her garden. She packed all her berries harvests to Spence's Bridge in cedar root baskets hung on the saddle horse, six miles downriver and those huge baskets to sell you know when we were little kids and she sell it and you know come home with store bought food in the baskets. So I think of what you say is right is witnessing the hard work that she you know some people might say, well, 'why do you Anderson girls know how to work', I think that's where it came from right there. The hard work, the work, we just worked because you had to because it was there and you never questioned it, everybody just worked hard on a daily basis (Trudine Dunstan, Personal Interview, 2010, p.2).

The *Nlakapmux* pedagogy for physical development included gathering and eating wholesome food and exercising well into elder years. Our Grandmothers also sang stories to us, over and over again to help us pick berries, then to put us to sleep at night. We all recalled the Owl story, when Granny sang, *"Neeshta schcoloola, Neeshta schcoloola, Neeshta schcoloola, Neeshta schcoloola,"* pointing to the skies for us to spot the *'schcoloola'* flying about in the mountains.

5.5.2 Spiritual Realm

Ceremony often was the demonstration of unity to the Great Spirit and represented the process of giving thanks/thanksgiving in order to have balance. The concept of balance is the goal of the Medicine Wheel wholistic framework. The development of the physical, mental and emotional self was accompanied by the *Nlakapmux* praxis for spiritual activities and many milestone ceremonies that included naming, rites for puberty, motherhood, and healing. Names were family property and signified family membership. Naming ceremonies marked these occasions and gave meaning to the child, family and community.

It was the custom in our *Nlakapmux* family to name the child at about one year of age, when the child could walk, as infant mortality was always a possibility.

That ceremony was called *Telehtc* (Standing Child up in front of the community). Children were named by the eldest matriarch of the family and names were chosen to prepare the child for her/his place in the family. Childhood names reflected the elements: water, spirit, and animals. Animals were usually boy names. Plants and birds were girl names. The name exemplified relationships in the extended family and relationships with the natural environment. Ceremonies that related to first achievements were also important.

There is time for celebration when an individual achieves a specific skill such as weaving her first cedar root basket. A ceremonial introduction of the newly woven basket and the use it is to provide to the family is part of the young girl's contribution and acknowledgement. Another important introductory ceremony occurred when a child was one year old, and given an *Nlakapmux* name as indicated earlier. When a child reached puberty, she/he participated in a vision quest and subsequent ceremony to mark this important milestone.

These practices were and continue to be valuable because they fulfill a specific purpose within the extended family. Celebrating life phases and accomplishments also instills in the individual a feeling of humility and gratitude to the Creator. One grandmother spoke about the relationship between the Creator, land, food, and teachings about how to treat others:

> Why are these important? Because I felt they were teaching me something I felt this was important that is why they were teaching me. They were trying to teach me something at the time, all the foods, where to pick it and to walk, not ride the horse. I said that prayer in the school when my daughter Angie asked me to say the prayer as I remembered, I said it like that. Translated it tells us to think good thoughts, love one another and the food blessing was *Katsa squest scooza yash aks shahsqu, kats melm sch-* lahunsh (Bless this food in the Creator's name and all will be good). We will eat and love one another after blessing the food. Why are these important enough? Because I felt they were teaching me something, I felt this was important, that is why they were teaching me, to pass it along. They were trying to teach me something at the time, all the foods, where to pick it and to walk, not ride the horse all the time (Lorna Sterling, Personal Interview, 2009, p.2).

In our historic past, opportunities for ceremonies were intricately woven into all life activities, which ensured that we were so intrinsically connected to our environments and to each other. Therefore, the transmission of Nlakapmux spiritual knowledge through ceremonial practices was an important means of acquiring ceremonial teachings, tribal epistemologies, and family, kinship and community histories. Death was another important time for ceremonies.

In my view, the remembrances around the death ceremony emerged and although referred to as a sad time for the family, even when very young, the children were taught that relatives, especially the old ones went to the spirit world. There were songs and talks that happened at the time of death, just as there were berry picking, hunting and travelling songs. Several Grandmothers (Verna B, Trudine D, Yvonne S) said that they learned that death is not good-bye but meant " I will be seeing you again someday " or " I will catch up with you someday."

> And I didn't understand why we were going home but when we got home I didn't know what it was then she was in a coffin in those days I can't remember, somebody made me look but I didn't want to look but I had to look. And I could still see this (Bernice Anderson, Personal Interview, 2010, p.4).

Our belief that we are all related to the mineral, plant, animal and human kingdoms sets the pedagogical foundation for everyday life and activities. A Grandmother stated "all creation had a value and we are to protect it by using everything usable, not to waste any part food or/of creation" (Trudine Dunstan, Personal Interview, 2010, p.2).

Ceremonies were a common way to teach spiritual lessons to children. They attended spiritual ceremonies from birth onward, often learning how to sit quietly until their turn to be involved. Sitting quietly could be considered a sacrifice for a young child. They also learned about spiritual matters through adult role modeling and learning interactions with their Grandmothers.

Sometimes, they may not have understood these practices or may have been somewhat frightened by them. However, they internalized these teachings to make sense of them later in life. Some of the Grandmothers shared such remembrances.

> I loved her Indian singing and her songs, She believed in the spirits coming and delivering things and placing something in the house, Lamiinak believed spirits came. I was scared of her, maybe she was trying to say goodbye. I used to sleep with her and she was getting old, and she died shortly after that. I was about 12 or so; she would sing Indian songs all night. Oh,[she would say] 'the spirit brought that here, shortly after Grandpa died'. She died in 1955. She believed spirits brought stuff to your human eye, and you could see and she did that, it was scary. She also believed she could make it rain!! I was too little. The cloudburst came because she believed you could make it rain by slapping two knives together and cutting the clouds (Lorna Sterling, Personal Interview, 2009, p.2).

And

> I still do the ceremonies. I am going to the Sundance, doing the fasting the time in June, yes, I think probably the whole thing about discipline, relationships and leadership and taking care of yourself, always a big thing for me. I do remember always, Granny Nancy saying the two words we don't say is "can't and won't." You can always do it, won't is disrespectful and when you say can't and as nothing is impossible, my own personal philosophy there is always a way and it is disrespectful to say I won't. 'Let's figure it out together,' I realized it is a generational thing, grandma saying that (Verna Billy-Minnabarriet, Personal Interview 2010, p.4).

Prayers and songs were shared at ceremonies, for birthing, naming, marriage, hunting and dying. Two Grandmothers described their spiritual learning relationship with their Grandmothers:

> When I come to about age three or four, I have recollections about mostly the sweat-baths with grandfather fire rocks, good porous rocks. She taught me prayers. The cleansing sweats began when I started dating and she explained that one's body parts had to be treated special and how to honor oneself...how to take care of oneself until one became married. I did these ceremonies with my daughter and nieces (Verna Billy-Minnabarriet, Personal Interview, 2010, p.4).

> Granny said always wash your face in cold water, it is healing and cleansing and empowering; it is also the best for keeping wrinkles away and after crying wash with cool water (Yvonne Shuter, Personal Interview, 2010, p.1).

When puberty was reached, an adult name was given to emphasize and continue

the development

the young adult's gifts.

5.5.3 Emotional Realm

During the process of making a cedar root basket one's emotional realm is challenged to persevere, especially if a part of the process becomes difficult. The basket maker had to realize that some things were 'tough,' but she had to finish the task. For instance, while gathering and preparing the cedar roots numerous trips were made to the cedar forest to harvest the straightest of roots; then the cherry bark from the wild cherry tree was harvested in the spring time when the sap was still running; a time consuming process that occurred over a one year period. This process taught us to be patient, flexible and tolerant. Our communion with the forest and partnering with her for these materials resulted in emotional strength and healing.

Weaving a coiled basket requires much dexterity and skill to fashion a receptacle to fulfill a specific purpose and it is like having emotional well-being and flexibility to fulfill our many roles in a family and community. Task fulfillment is one goal of emotional stability. A second goal stemming from emotional stability is the ability to learn a new technique, such as weaving a uniform coil on a basket or telling a story over and over again until it is told correctly. A third goal for emotional stability is sharing work with others, and embracing new materials or processes as a natural part of change; the realization that we do not need to complete a job alone but be able to accept help along the way is a sign of emotional maturity.

Completing the most difficult task under trying circumstances and persevering to the end are values which are integral to wholistic development. The development of a woman's discipline (to carry out one's roles and responsibilities) begins at puberty, when the girl is honored and taught how to care for herself to develop her confidence and self-reliance. All my Grandmother participants remembered the practices introduced at puberty ceremonies with spiritual prayers and vision questing that prepared girls to become fully functioning women. Several of the participants gave examples of their emotional development and how they learned to persevere with any task: "*Petensh aks yeas* as *chahchawoot (Think in a good way about your work) and you'll* love it" (Lorna Sterling, Personal Interview, 2010, p.2).

Patsy McKay emphasized her coming of age in learning:

> *A zzoomt a schmoolatch* (menses) they take the pubescent girl to bathe in the river and run to the top of the mountain and poke pine needles in your arm pits so we can't have an odor. She taught me cultural knowledge which I taught my kids, and if I deviate, they now correct me (Patsy McKay, Personal Interview, 2010, p.2).

And yet another shared her emotional learnings:

> Grandma Nancy had shared with me about puberty rites...able to tell me all the way through, also the work ethics, about family connections, who your people were. I feel I got the privileges as the oldest girl. I got to be grandma's girl. The thing about those transition teachings, maybe, could be, more complete, my good fortune, being older, just like your younger sisters couldn't remember details. I probably had more opportunity to interact one to one with grandmas, because mom and dad were busy raising kids, I had Grandmothers Nancy and Mary who emphasized getting an education and going to school as paramount importance and I, in turn saying to my kids the same thing, and saying to them; you don't need that addiction that drink\or smoke or any excesses (Verna Billy-Minnabarriet, Personal Interview, 2010, p.2).

In a traditional community and extended family context, Grandmothers were the caregivers and teachers, while mothers worked on tanning deer hides and gathering food. Grandmothers took their time, caring for the children, walking slowly, so little kids could keep up, talking and storytelling and picking berries or medicine plants, children helped, filling their small baskets for Grandmother. As the girls grew older their Grandmothers created opportunities for the important spiritual ceremonies: discipline and womanhood training began in earnest at puberty and continued for one year. Nothing was explained until that time arrived, and then explicit instructions were given and shown.

Each and every Grandmother had vivid memories of their first 'zoomt'\or moontime (menstrual cycle). These lessons and teachings would sustain her through the various phases of life: preparation for marriage, childbirth, motherhood, for living a good life and for passing to the next world. Remembering that all life was interconnected, learnings and teachings were for the woman, and grandmother within family and community. Thus, cycle teachings were deliberately performed through life phases. This was of paramount importance as the grandmother was the head of the matriarchal clan of the nation and she held the Indigenous knowledge through experience and practice.

The Grandmothers' remembrances of women's practices were sometimes fragmented or fractured; however, a common practice included rising early, before the "crack of dawn" and running to the water to bathe, in a creek, lake, stream or river.

> Girls were assigned tasks, and to complete them no matter how tedious, and to clean themselves and strengthen themselves by prayer when afraid (Verna Billy-Minnabarriet, Personal Interview, 2010, p.1).

Another traditional teaching for young girls menstruating for the first time became evident as I continued my documentation:

> At puberty, we had to run fast down the road, you would be a fast runner, pick fruit fast, you would be fast all your life!! (Lorna Sterling, Personal Interview, 2009, p.2).

The disciplinary practices conveyed during this moon time period assisted the girls to transition from childhood to womanhood, effortlessly without emotional incongruity. These passages were part of life and they were acknowledged through ceremonies. The young girls learned their various roles as they transitioned to adulthood. It is my belief that we as women and Grandmothers have a stronger link to our responsibilities because of our knowledge of these practices. Our emotional development was closely associated with our mental development.

5.5.4 Mental Realm

Mental engagement, prior to and during cedar root basket making, ensures that the correct materials, weaving designs, and shapes are planned before making the chosen basket. The mental realm focuses on cultural learning and is a lifelong process: from cradle to grave. Storytelling was a way of teaching while carrying out daily activities that created the ability for growing children to develop thinking skills that involved problem solving, analysis, and critical engagement.

These stories were and are often infused with many other concepts, information and most importantly kinship knowledge. Often the listener had to reflect and dissect the story to develop understandings that prepared her/him for their life journey. The following characteristics influenced the quality of lifelong learning: versatility, creativity, and inter-generational learning and teachings.

> When my grandbaby was born I made his cradle board, remembering, when Kris and Heidi, my kids, were born, mom helped me or I helped her collect the materials to make the cradle board, so I relied on that information and remembered how I as a child with grandma Nancy making Uncle Harold's oldest daughter a cradle board Nancy and I was asking Harold to go and help us find it and she was talking about making the board, sour cherry tree, light and strong, it was cherry wood (Verna Billy-Minnabarriet, Personal Interview, 2010 p. 3).

The *Nlakapmux* were known for their style and expertise as coil basket makers, which was a common method of basketry among the Interior Salish. This acknowledgment of expertise was transferred to the younger generation and ensured that the art continued, but more importantly it was a distinctive identity that was used to establish the Nlakapmux women as experts and the baskets as valuable for family/community sustenance and trade items.

The basket making process infused the ability to problem solve, to become an expert, revealing the specialty of the individual and reinforcing their worth and personal power. Pedagogy related to cedar root basket making included developing memory and listening skills and learning how to make tools with natural things such as bone awls from deer. Baskets were also made from pine needles and bear grass. The Grandmothers also learned to make buckskin clothing, moccasins, and gloves from deer hides; dyes from plants; necklaces from seeds; and baby cradleboards from birch bark.

> The development of the mind was holistically intertwined and woven into activities and stories shared by the grandmothers on a daily basis. Grandmothers shared the transmission of knowledge or mental teachings they learned as children and are learning today (Trudine Dunstan, Personal Interview, 2010, p.4).

Grandmothers remembered the lasting impact of experiential learning and storytelling in response to knowledge or mental teachings.

> As a child picking the bitter roots and learning about the ancestral Bigfoot and other stories while picking and cleaning roots still echo in my mind (L. Sterling, Personal Interview, 2009.P.2).

Grandmother Patsy described her experiences food gathering with her Grandmother:

> And, we used to fix bitter root, digging bitter root and when we were little, the people would go by horseback in *Petani (Botani)*, single file on horseback, all manner of our natural foods are found in *Petani*, it is now called nature's garden, because we still go there today, however the men

> hunted for deer and the old ladies and kids dug *tatoon* or wild potatoes (Patsy McKay, Personal Interview, 2009, p.2).

In addition to being basket makers, women usually were keepers of the medicinal, plant and food knowledge that included processes for gathering, cleaning and preserving food. Historically cedar root baskets were a valuable bartering item, emphasizing the worth of the basket maker which gave women power.

The prevalent currency in my growing up years was food grown for sustenance. All through my school years, my parents traded bounty from our garden and orchard for room and board in an adjacent town in order for my siblings and I to attend public school. So too, trading or bartering for every day transportation was learned, as the following Grandmother describes;

> I learned about bartering from Grandma Nancy when it came time to go to Ashcroft. We had to catch the Greyhound bus and if she had no money, we would arise at 4 am, in the morning. Granny picked three boxes of tomatoes, put these by the highway spot and we got ready for town then stood there. The driver Mr. Clark, the bus driver, would stop and, he called her Mrs. Nancy and she told him the tomatoes were our fare, sometimes Grandmother gave him buckskin gloves she had made in winter, bartering with Mr. Clark, that is how grandma paid for the fare. We wanted to go and come back, not only one-way and he made sure we got home. In winter we went to Cache Creek, sometimes she gave two pairs of gloves and dry meat and we got on the bus. He was very happy and so were we (Verna Billy-Minnabarriet, Personal Interview 2010, p.3).

Other teachings recalled by the *Nlakapmux* Grandmothers included how experience and direct participation were the ways and means of transferring ancestral knowledge; in this process the learnings were everlasting and transported to the next generation.

> Great grandmother Alice always showed us how the food grew in the garden. We would pick it together and then go home and cook. Alice used to make moccasins out of old jeans. She used coyote fur to trim them. She made a lot of these denim slippers; in hindsight it took improvisation to do that (Lorna Sterling, Personal Interview, 2009, p.2).

The art of storytelling was always a very natural process while travelling, picking berries and visiting Grandmothers. The lessons for mental development included preparing and teaching us how to improvise with the inclusion of creative storytelling when we would ask questions about "Bigfoot" calling on our imaginary processes to think about where 'Bigfoot" lived and what he did for an occupation and whether or not he might like children to accompany, work or play with him.

As we grew older, Grandmothers told us stories over and over again to stay close to home and to care for one another, usually the eldest child was made responsible for the care and safety of the younger siblings. The Grandmothers recalled the 'Bigfoot" story. When Granny told and sang *"Quanata tsamoolaawhh, Quanata tsamoolaawhh, Quanata tsamoolaawhh, Quanata tsamoolaawhh,"* she pointed to the big door shape etched into the adjacent mountain for us to spot the entry way to Bigfoot's dwelling place. During childhood, urgings for children to stay close to home were imparted by stories, such as:

> The Bigfoot was the scariest story she told the most. She said do not go riding by yourself to the other ranch, you see that big rock over there is where the Bigfoot lives, and she would point to a door looking indent in the big rock (Lorna Sterling, Personal Interview, 2009, p.3).

Developing our imaginations, and combining thinking lessons, decision-making and creative play were enduring *Nlakapmux* pedagogy for the mental realm.

5.6 Summary of *Nlakapmux* Grandmother Perspectives

The findings about the Grandmothers' perspectives were organized using the Medicine Wheel's four realms of physical, spiritual, emotional, and mental development. In a description of the Medicine Wheel, one's journey includes the child, youth, young adult and Elder phases. The teachings are specific to each phase and are not necessarily completed before moving on to the next phase. Especially in today's world, one's life journey has many gifts for each direction and it is our challenge to continue and persevere in the lessons presented.

In my *Nlakapmux* ways of knowing I illustrate my Grandmother perspectives in the four realms as spiritual opposite physical, and emotional opposite mental realms. I understand there is tension between the physical and spiritual realms. When we are born we are in the physical realm and as we age we develop spiritually becoming the wise Elder. When we are young we are in the emotional realm and maturing into the mental realm. The flexibility of the Medicine Wheel as an illustrative tool for my Grandmother *Nlakapmux* concepts is displayed in Figure 7 below. I have illustrated my Grandmother perspectives in these four realms, recognizing there is overlap into the realms, which is unavoidable.

Figure 7. *Nlakapmux* Perspectives' Wheel

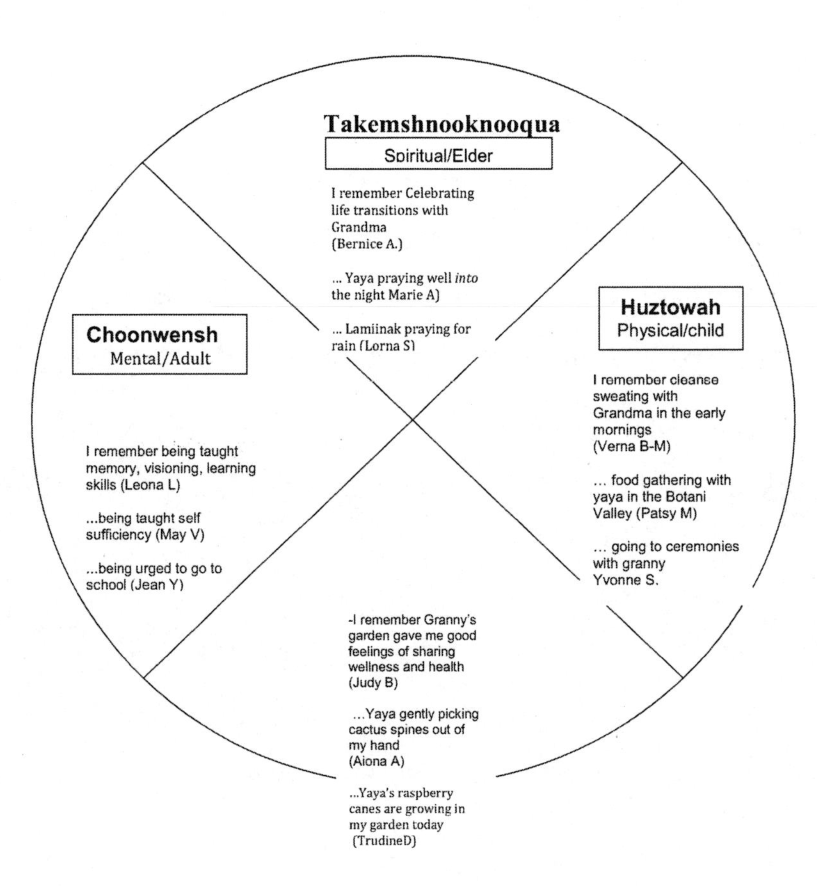

It is significant to discern the activities of each Medicine Wheel realm leading to the wholistic development of the child. This promotes learning of the heart, mind, body, and spirit. The learning and teaching experiences between Grandmother and grandchildren creates a nurturing relationship in which the children develop an ability to inter-relate with their environments, Grandmothers, family and community. This is demonstrated by the *Nlakapmux* Grandmother perspectives, which I believe formulated the learning and teaching praxes and pedagogy of our oral society. The fundamental premise is that each person is his or her own teacher, teaching and learning through the role modeling behavior of the Grandmother. These *Nlakapmux* concepts form the very foundation of the cedar root basket metaphor that is illustrated further in the next chapter.

In weaving a cedar root basket, the beginning part is the formation of the bottom of the basket, which determines the size and shape of the basket. The foundation of the basket needs to be sturdy and strong to fulfil its function. But even before this stage occurs the resources, roots, design material and tools are identified and found. When the weaver has everything ready, the basket may begin to be woven. The structure of the basket is made row by row, ascending from the foundation and according to the planned use of the basket tightness of the weave, shape and height and design are determined. Once the basket weaving starts, it is important to complete the basket in a timely way so that the shape, color and uniformity of the work will be consistent in order to produce an exemplary product.

Chapter Six: *Caustem* (Using) *Nlakapmux* Teachings and Learnings

This chapter addresses the remaining *Shinkyap shau'a'tem – thesis research questions:*

- Which Nlakapmux teachings and pedagogies are practiced in the Grandmothers' families today?
- What are the challenges and opportunities for continuing these Nlakapmux teachings and pedagogies in family and community settings?

Chapter Five focused on Grandmothers' traditional pedagogical experiences and relationships they had with their Grandmothers. Wholistic learning that addressed their physical, spiritual, emotional, and mental development was exemplified. I used the metaphor of cedar root basket making to make meaning of the Grandmothers stories and perspectives. In this chapter, I have woven the concepts, the teachings and learnings together in order to demonstrate a theoretical way of understanding and then using them. The *Nlakapmux* concept of *caustem* - our use of them (pedagogy and praxis) - helped me to create an *Nlakapmux Developing Wisdom Theory* (NDWT).

6.1 *Nlakapmux*: Developing Wisdom Theory

The cedar root basket becomes a symbol for holding and using this particular *Nlakapmux* theory (see Figure 8). The principles are strands that have a distinct meaning. They are woven into a material object that has historical, contemporary, and future value which functions to help people live a better life. The recurring themes from the Grandmothers' individual interviews and group circle dialogue form the basis of the eight principles that my *Nlakapmux* family and some community Grandmothers utilize as foundations for living a good life.

The discussions of these principles/theory are intertwined with stories, histories, and lessons that delineate what and how the Grandmothers transfer Indigenous Knowledge in order to develop wisdom, which is a lifelong process. In addition, elements of my personal lived experience story and pertinent literature are woven into this theoretical framework.

I believe that these principles have been used and reinforced in our oral society through the telling and retellings of stories, so that the stories become the basis of teachings and learnings that solidify what being *Nlakapmux* is, what it means and how one becomes *Nlakapmux*. I agree with Archibald's statement about the influence of Indigenous stories upon our identities as "ways to help people think, feel, and 'be' through the power of stories" (2008, p. 84). The eight *Nlakapmux* transformational pedagogical principles emerging from the Grandmother stories and literature include:

- *Takemshooknooqua*, Knowing we are connected: land, animals, plants and people;
- *ChaaChawoowh*, Celebrating people and land joyously;
- *Huckpestes*, Developing lifelong learning and wisdom;
- Huztowaahh, Giving lovingly to family and community;
- *Choownensh*, Succeeding in endeavours;
- *Choowaachoots*, Utilizing Nlakapmux vision-seeking methods;
- *Nmeenlth coynchoots*, Incorporating Nlakapmux knowledge; and
- *Peteenushem*, Reflecting on learning and relearning lifelong lessons.

In the following figure I have displayed these eight concepts on the cedar root basket to illustrate the intricate design of *Nlakapmux* teachings and learnings that form my *Nlakapmux Developing Wisdom Theory*. The *Nlakapmux* Medicine Basket also contains or holds the Grandmothers' wholistic spiritual, emotional, physical and mental teachings and learnings. A more comprehensive explanation of each strand follows Figure 8[4]

Figure 8. *Nlakapmux* Developing Wisdom Theory

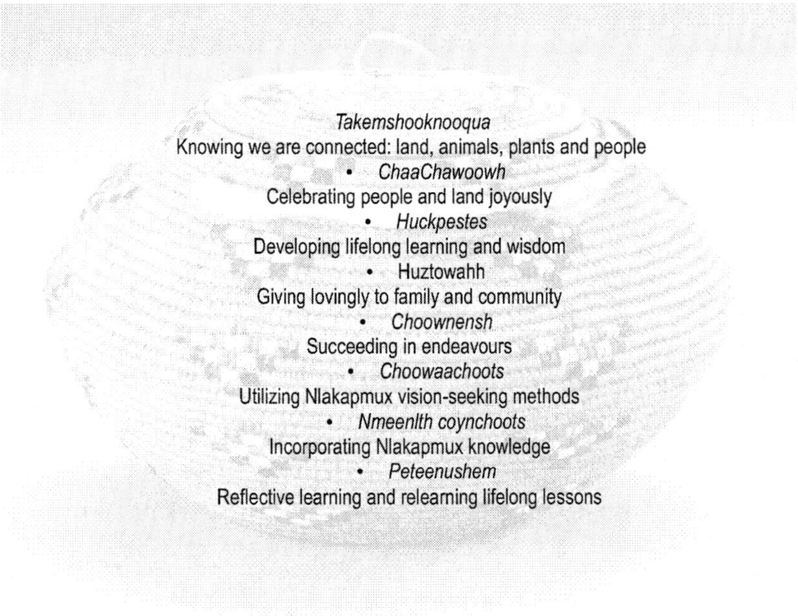

Takemshooknooqua
Knowing we are connected: land, animals, plants and people

- *ChaaChawoowh*
  Celebrating people and land joyously
- *Huckpestes*
  Developing lifelong learning and wisdom
- Huztowahh
  Giving lovingly to family and community
- *Choownensh*
  Succeeding in endeavours
- *Choowaachoots*
  Utilizing Nlakapmux vision-seeking methods
- *Nmeenlth coynchoots*
  Incorporating Nlakapmux knowledge
- *Peteenushem*
  Reflective learning and relearning lifelong lessons

[4] The image of the *Nlakapmux* cedar root basket is printed with permission from the Canadian Museum of Civilization. The basket maker is unknown.

6.2 *Takemshooknooqua*: Knowing We are Connected - Land, Animals, Plants, and People

This principle forms an epistemological foundational for the *Nlakapmux* people. It focuses on our relationship to all of creation. *Takemshnooqua* literally means 'all my relations.' Therefore, inherent in those few words in our language resides the understandings we have about all our relationships, seen and unseen. We intrinsically understand that we are connected to minerals, plants, animals and humans. I believe that our language holds many answers about life and living on the landscape of our territories. There are important teachings about the landscape, the wild plants, animals, and family connections and genealogies.

Stories common in our territory include the customs of our people to live in harmony with Earth Mother, doing no harm to her, harvesting food with permission, and practicing gratitude and reverence. Our people thank the bird, plant and animal spirits for sacrificing their lives to sustain us. The Grandmother interviewees remembered, "We were taught not to kill bugs, birds or little animals" (Judy B) and "We were taught that all of creation had value and we were to protect it by using everything usable; not to waste any plant part for food or buckskin for clothing" (Verna B, Trudine D).

Similarily, all our community members were regarded as close relatives and treated accordingly with love, *huztoowah.* Lessons for sharing were demonstrated early in our childhoods as the Grandmothers remembered; when passers by were invited in for a meal, not just tea (Lorna S, Trudine D). I believe that we were taught this value and teaching starting at childhood by role modelling from our grandmothers.

We were taught to help our Grandmothers by getting tea for them at meal time or in between meals. The young family members who served their Grandmothers were invited to join them, which created a special bond between Grandmother and child. One Grandmother remembered a china cup her Grandmother had gifted her when she was very little. Her Grandmother purchased the china tea cup and saucer from a travelling salesman. She purchased it especially for her second oldest granddaughter. Every time the grandaughter (now a Grandmother) made tea at her Grandmother's house the special china tea cup was used, thus becoming their ritual (Jean Y). The special learning relationship between a Grandmother and her grandchildren was an important pedagogical process that instilled environmental knowledge and values of sharing and caring for others.

Each of the Grandmother interviewees spoke of their current practice of taking only what was needed when harvesting food. For example: leaving berries on the bush for other birds or people; when picking medicinal plants taking a few leaves from a number of plants rather then taking the whole plant; and when preparing salmon or fish cooking all its parts, including the head and roe (Leona L, Trudine D, Verna B).

In my experience, the pedagogical principle of 'we are all related' was inherent in *Nlakapmux* knowledge. We are part of an intrinsic whole, in essence it is the knowledge linking us to the cosmos and each other. I understood this concept from observing and learning from my Grandmother. She created opportunities to share with her family, growing food, making clothes and sharing all she had with any member of the community. When we say *takemshnooqua*, we are remembering all our relatives, human, non-human, current and ancestral, calling on them all, during every waking moment and in prayers.

Current day uses for this principle of *takemshnooqua* may be applied to any developments pertaining to our environments, to our family and community, and to our children's schooling. In the school community we could complement existing curriculua and extra-curricular activities with *Nlakapmux* ways to teach *takemshnooqua.*

We must continue to support each other emotionally, spiritually, physically, and mentally in family and community contexts. This principle emphasizes the teaching that we need each other to survive and thrive. I imagine that *takemshnooqua,* if practiced today, would help overcome negative family and community interactions of greed, 'backbiting', and jealousy, which have emerged over the years.

6.3 *ChaaChawoowh*: Celebrating People and Land Joyously

Indigenous scholar Jo-ann Archibald (1997) developed a Coast Salish Indigenous theoretical storywork framework for pedagogy and methodology. She also evoked the presence of Coyote the trickster through stories, analysis, and reflection. In Archibald's scholarship Coyote and those reading her work learn to make a storybasket through understanding these principles: respect, responsibility, reverence, reciprocity, wholism, inter-relatedness, and synergy. The Elders with whom Archibald learned shared many examples of story related pedagogy that they experienced.

One example that resonates with me was when one of my Grandmother participants stated the their grandmother often asked them to repeat the story next time. Archibald shared that in her work she encountered this same response when the Elder asks the child to repeat the story "back" to the Elder to see if she did indeed understand the story (Archibald, 2008, p. 134). Many Grandmother stories were about the Indigenous names for land/nature and relationships to places that created a special kinship to them (Verna B, Judy B.). In my experience a child reacts *chaachhaawuh,* joyously to be asked by the Elder to tell the story "back" because she can excel at this task and at the same time develop a special kinship to the Elder and to land/nature.

This *Nlakapmux* concept, *chaachaawoowh*, describes the happiness felt by one to be wholly present, to utilize all senses, and to be joyous in the moment. This teaching is about being in the 'here and now': not to dwell on past issues but to realize that each day brings a new beginning. Creating rejoiceful moments to be with someone, a grandchild, parent or friend, is part of the meaning of this concept. When one is *chaachawoowh,* it is an opportunity to begin anew without the baggage of previous days. Our Grandmothers demonstrated this quality by their expression of joy when they first saw us at birth.

This joy continued throughout our growing years. This joyous quality encompasses others and other activities. It is to rejoice in one another's presence. It is giving full attention to our present company. My mother exuded this quality. She was genuine and in the moment, throughout her life. Another key word to use is 'our' which implies a significant connection to the extended family and our community.

Chaachawoowh is to be joyful in the knowledge that we are alive, that we belong, and that we can learn. A sense of joy among Elders is evident even in the face of genocide. Despite our colonized history, they never stopped caring for their families. Other examples of *chaachaawoowh* are evident when Grandmothers walked on the land to pick wild plants to eat or to use for medicine for family members. They were joyous because they knew they could provide what was needed for their family and community members. Some of the Grandmothers still experience the joyous connection between gathering resources from the land for their family and community (Verna B, Trudine D, Patsy M, Judy B.).

Traditionally, one who practiced *chaachaawoowh* was thankful for and greeted the new day, a new member, a visiting family as well as the arrival of fresh meat or salmon. This enduring quality was shared with everyone. *Nlakapmux* knowledge transmission, occurred naturally or organically and, as mentioned in the previous chapter, ceremonies were an important pedagogical means for knowledge transmission.

Knowing that we are a tribal people has created distinctness from the mainstream Western society; therefore, the concept of c*haachaawoowh* has a deeper meaning then being in a family, per se. To be joyful in the knowledge that we belong to a collective is reassuring and important to us. Some of our teachings are similar to other Indigenous groups such as the following quote about Okanagan Indigenous learning described by Indigenous scholar Bill Cohen:

> The external assessors were privileged and honoured to have had the opportunity to observe Okanagan Language instruction during morning class...The energy, high expectations for learning, and lesson planning provided by Chad Marchand the young adult teacher was exemplary. The presence of a guiding Elder, the strong support provided by the two non-Native teachers, the determination and the pure joy [*chaachaawoowh*] demonstrated by 20 students during an intense 90 minutes of instruction was outstanding (2010, p.272).

The quote above indicates the *Nlakapmux* principle of *chaachawoowh* to be present in our neighbouring Okanagan tribe's contemporary pedagogy.

Today, *chaachaawoowh* pedagogy can be and indeed is carried out through ceremonies such as those for 'Naming.' These ceremonies are a means of validating Nlakapmux identity and connections to land and environment. Most importantly they are joyous occasions. In order to have a successful Naming ceremony, family members need to work together and to do it with hope, joy and love for the children or young people being named.

Today, Naming ceremonies include a giveaway, which may require a one-year family planning process. Gifts are given to guests, and to community members who have helped the family. During the giveaway, the host family shares their joy, tangibly. The ceremony provides a pedagogical framework for gifting, giving hospitality, giving the name, strengthening kinship, giving thanks, giving prayers, sharing stories to help one through life's incidents, and giving hope for a brighter future to the family and community: in essence, *chaachaawoowh.*

6.4 *Huckpestes*: Developing Life-long Learning and Wisdom

The key word here is 'wisdom' or the development of wisdom, which is the accumulation of a lifetime of lived experiences where one reflects critically upon them. This means that we learn from our experiences from birth onward. Therefore a child displays wisdom when he/she learns from and does not repeat a self-defeating behaviour. *Huckpestes* occurs when one engages in a critical analysis, reaches a different decision, and alters her behaviour accordingly. I heard a story once, the teller said, "I was walking down the road to my destination and fell into a big hole. The next day I tried again, taking the same road to reach my destination. I again fell into the big hole." A wise person responded, "Take a different road." We have to find our road, and through experience and gradually developing wisdom, an Elder may find the 'good' choice of roads and be considered a wisdom holder. This recognition is reflected in the concept of living a 'Good Life,' which was a lifelong learning goal.

In my memories and based on my research analysis and findings I realize and recognize that our Grandmothers never ceased learning nor transmitting knowledge to their families and community. For example, the value of cleanliness is not only a physical teaching but encompasses the wholistic teaching of care for self in the four realms that were discussed in the previous chapter. The following Grandmother's quote shows that sometimes the teachings were carried out in an implicit manner:

> Yeah. That's some of the things I remember. I don't necessarily well I guess it's well it is teachings, even though I wasn't told in particular that they taught me but again I remember cleanliness and I guess being particular (Trudine Dunstan, Interview, 2010, p.2).

The example about cleanliness was a common one for our family of girls. My memories of Grandmother *Yaya* are vivid of her sweeping the ground in front of the little log house, so the little ones would stay clean; cleaning the dishes, cleaning the barn, cleaning our clothes, and also cleaning our mind of frivolity when berry picking was to be done. The Grandmothers remembered another meaning to the phrase, "cleaning house," which referred to keeping away from bad habits such as smoking and drinking. Learning to be 'clean' and healthy was a lifelong process where many self-discoveries were possible.

A new found awareness could also be referred to as *huckpestena,* which means *discoveries.* My Grandmother interviewees shared stories of their discoveries; some of which happened later in their lives. These new discoveries or "awarenesses" occurred through reflection; confirming my developing wisdom theory. Several Grandmothers shared the practice of "never being allowed to sleep over at another's house. My grandmother protected me" (Trudine D, Verna B, Aiona A). In practicing *huckpestena* or discovery, we recognize opportunity of choices to be made, in these cases the Grandmothers appreciated the facts after they discovered why they were not allowed to overnite elsewhere. In another example, I recall the acquisition of a second vehicle in our family when the youngest son went to school. I took a paying job. I needed a second car to get to work, however, the second car also brought separate trips outside of work, an unexpected consequence, in hindsight, *huckpestena,* a contributing factor to separating the family unit where we no longer travelled together.

Grandmothers' wisdom is still central to many First Nations' extended families despite the many social and societal transitions that have occurred (Alfred, 2004; Archibald, 1997; Battiste, & Barman, 1995; Gardner, 2000). A growing body of literature talks about First Nations' Elder Teachings (Archibald, 2008; Gardner, 2000; Sam, 2001 & Sterling, 1997). These scholars discuss and illustrate Grandmother Teachings or lessons, but what is usually left unsaid is the Grandmothers' "teaching practice" or praxis stemming from their Indigenous language. My thesis identifies, describes and documents *Nlakapmux* Indigenous Grandmothers' teaching practices using *Nlakapmux* concepts and language to illustrate authentically emerging *Nlakapmux* pedagological principles and the developing wisdom theory.

The oral practice of *huckpestes* develops wisdom through intergenerational learning and storytelling and reflection, beginning with the *Nlakapmux* child, and extends outward to *Nlakapmux* family, extended family and commmunity (see Figure 9). Intergenerational storytelling has been the means of oral knowledge transmission for *Nlakapmux* people; this practice incorporates all the wholistic learning senses for children and gradually was replaced by organized school and written English words. Traditionally storytelling was the natural pedagogy to guide the growth and development for the children within their *Nlakapmux* community as the following diagram represents.

Figure 9. *Nlakapmux* Intergenerational Learning

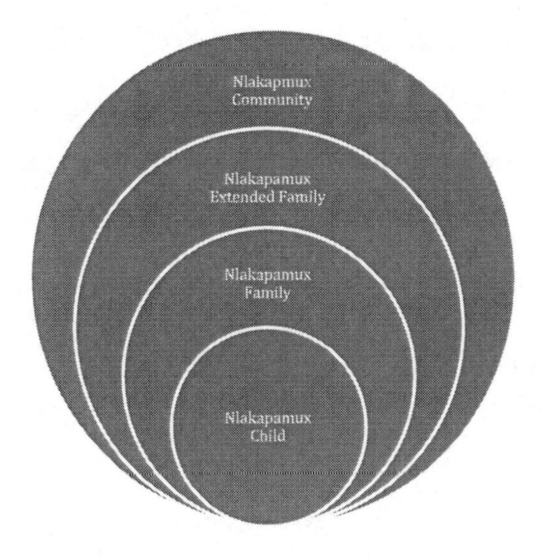

In contrast, *Nlakapmux* scholar Shirley Sterling uses a different story telling approach that exemplifies the lifelong impact of intergenerational stories in her doctoral thesis (1997). She writes about *Skaloola,* the Owl. She first tells the story of the Owl snatching children up to take to his house. She tells the story and the subsequent actions of the children, the older kids, and the parents.

The story affects each generation differently, but she also describes outcomes resulting from the story. Some examples of the interactions include: the little children were listened to as they described the owl they saw; and the older kids saw the story somewhat like their parents, as a form of social control, keeping the children close to home and in the parents' absence also getting the children to go to bed. Sterling added other story meanings which may include a form of protection from marauding tribes or perhaps preventing children from wandering off or putting themselves in danger. The story serves as a conversational starter for the extended family and even the community as it is a story all members know and have utilized intergenerationally.

6.5 *Huztowaahh*: Giving Lovingly to Family and Community

The concept of huztowaahh, describes the practice of loving the extended family as well as the collective community to which one belongs. We were taught not to bear ill will toward anyone in our family or community member.

We were encouraged to show respect and to develop close relationships with community members, in essence to treat them as part of our extended family.

Children were regarded as precious gifts and were loved, unconditionally, by all members of the community. Grandparents and extended family members helped raise the children. One Grandmother participant mentioned that her older sister was raised by one of her Grandmothers. There were many reasons for taking care of grandchildren, which included: one family may not have had many children and could help out or family members with many children had difficulty providing for all their children.

To instill the value of sharing and demonstrating care for others, children were taught to give away the first object they made, be it a basket, a drum, a sketch, or a garment. In my own memory, there was an incident at age nine, where I received two Betty dolls at Christmas; I was encouraged to give one of them to another girl, not in my immediate family.

Children, parents and grandparents living together within the village supported one another with all their daily needs. It was customary to look after the Elders of a tribe, giving them the choicest cuts of meat, fish, and fruit. Family and community members readily shared their catch of game and salmon, along with grown produce (Patsy M, Verna B, Lorna S).

The concept of huztowaahh was not practiced by everyone in a family after contact. Shirley Sterling's (1992) scholarship regarding two *Nlakapmux* Grandmother pedagogical models for education is an example. She expounds at length about the educational approaches of her two Grandmothers. Sterling recognizes *Yetco* her maternal Grandmother for keeping her generous extended family pedagogy by giving generously to her extended family and others. Having *Nlakapmux* huztowaahh pedagogy encourages young people (learners), and their family and community members (teachers) to practice unconditional acceptance, and to develop trust in order to learn and teach effectively. Approaching students with 'open arms and recognizing their gifts' creates meaningful results (Verna B, Yvonne S. Judy B.)

In keeping with huztowaahh , I believe unconditional regard (non-judgmental) and love are essential for creating an environment for quality education to take place. In my experience when one is in an environment where there is total acceptance without any judgements, the opportunity for creativity is present. This environment allows one to expound on theory building or theory making without fear of rejection, therefore, obtaining optimum thinking. In a book called *Shinwauk's Vision*, J. R. Miller (1997) writes of the three 'L's 'necessary for Aboriginal children to learn in the classroom.

> The various educational practices of the Aboriginal populations shared a common philosophical or spiritual orientation, as well as a similar approach. For all these peoples, instruction was suffused with their deeply ingrained spirituality, an invariable tendency to relate the material and personal in their lives to the spirits and the unseen. Moreover, they all emphasized an approach to instruction that relied on looking, listening and learning – the three L's (Miller, 1943.p.16)[5].

I elaborate on his theory to add a fourth L - Love. This is necessary as the element of unconditional love was removed from our family practices due to the historical attempts of systemic genocide through enforced Residential School attendance. Cajete's pedagogical model of "learning how to learn" (1995, p. 223) is based on the cultivation of the human capacities of listening, observing, experiencing with all one's senses; developing intuitive understanding; and respecting successful traditions of learning. Cajete further elaborates that many tribal societies consisted of a continuum of education that involved ritual/initiatory practices that celebrated various phases of human development.

[5] Traditional Native education was described as the three L's – look, listen and learn-' by 'Mark' a young man who appeared in the *Our Stories* episode on *Yukon Outfitter Johnny Johns*, CBC-TV, 5 July 1994 (Miller (1943, p. 445)

During each phase, learning how to learn was internalized within our families of origin. Cajete (1997) identifies four phases of orientation which are comprised of (1) learning how to survive purposefully; (2) allowing individuals to develop self-reliance and determination; (3) encouraging flexibility, viability and effectiveness; and (4) honouring and facilitating the transformational processes. Cajete's theory speaks to me as an *Nlakapmux* tribal person, as I have uncovered my Grandmothers' teachings, which also incorporates and expands similar ideas.

6.6 *Choonwensh*: Succeeding in Endeavours

The *Nlakapmux* concept of *choownensh* focuses on creating conditions for successful learning. *Choonwensh* synthesises all our practices for wholistic development (spiritual, emotional, physical and mental) and it is essential to the success of an individual/self, family and community. Much of our important *Nlakapmux* knowledge is passed on through family and community interactions during storytelling and in every day living in extended families.

All of the developmental stages of the child, teen, young adult, mature adult and finally Elder, require teachings. Grandmothers as Elders form a critical part of our extended family network and they play a vital role in the transmission of

Indigenous knowledge from one generation to another. They guide individuals through their life phases and are active family care givers and teachers. Today many Grandmothers still live with their children, grandchildren, and great-grandchildren. They may take on major responsibilities for raising their grandchildren. The oldest Grandmother participant is 89 years old. She commented, "I raised my granddaughter when my son died and I am now raising her child as she is not able to do that" (May V). Another Grandmother participant fondly recalled her intergenerational learning interactions where cultural knowledge was lived with her grandmother:

> Memorable times…being taught cultural knowledge by all of them. I learned lots from Grandma Nancy, my great Grandmother; she was my dad's granny, from when I came to live with her. [It was] when I first had memory, about 5 years old….[I remember] Grandma Nancy and later Grandma Mary, in their sweat house, we did sweats. I always thought Grandma Nancy was so wise until I went with Mary, who also talked about earth connections and how you are connected to animals and the land and yourself (Verna B. Interview, 2010,p.4).

In our group discussions we pondered: What is success? How is it measured? Is it a success to recognize the values upheld by the Grandmothers? How are these values demonstrated and recognized? We agreed that to reach *choonwensh*\success is when we are able to replicate the actions of *huztoowah* (extended family and community love) of long ago, *huckpestes* (lifelong learning), and *chaachawoowh* (validating tribal people and land connections).

This philosophical discussion of our *Nlakapmuxcin* concepts conveyed the deeper meanings of our Grandmothers' wisdom theory development.

Despite the infiltration of written English and its dominance over the *Nlakapmux* language, some Grandmothers still demonstrated oral ancestral knowledge in *Nlakapmuxcin* that they learned from their Grandmothers. The Grandmother participants spoke of the continuation of *Nlakapmux* thought by demonstrating their knowledge of the language and the incorporation of *Nlakapmux* philosophy and beliefs in their everyday lives. One Grandmother spoke proudly about the raspberry plants that she maintained over the years, which were obtained from the same garden as her great Grandmother. This example shows success in keeping plant knowledge 'alive'.

This same Grandmother has given her grandchildren *Nlakapmux* ancestral registered names, with the eldest turning 16 this year. To her, we say *choonwensh*. She has succeeded with the action of bestowing traditional names, which is a move toward traditionalism. And in our discussion, we also questioned how to keep traditional teachings such as *choonwensh* present on a daily basis, when the modern world with its competing demands is upon us? Once more, in drawing on Teit's recorded story and in my remembering how I was told the story, we returned to the power of *Shinkyap*/Coyote stories to help us with these questions.

6.6.1 "The Poor Hunter Story" as told by *Shinkyap*/Coyote

A poor hunter was left behind by his tribal members and given only one arrow. *Shinkyap*/Coyote told the poor hunter that he was to follow these instructions next time he went hunting. He was to go to a particular gulch and fire his one arrow high in the air and to let it land in the gulch. Upon going to retrieve the arrow, the hunter saw that the arrow had penetrated four deer, all simultaneously. From that day forward, he became known as a great hunter (Nlakapmux oral story).

The telling and retelling of stories are opportunities to recapture the essence of the magic of Coyote and transformation stories. This genre of stories teaches indirectly in a non-threatening way, allowing the listeners to come to their own solution and decisions. Indirect learning and teaching is a 'face saving' strategy and a part of *Nlakapmux* pedagogy. This face saving measure is common and shown in our stories during times of distress and poverty. No one is judged to be lazy or a "no-account" because they are a poor hunter.

In this ancestral *Shinkyap*/Coyote story a poor hunter can become successful with the help of friends, family, and community. Some of the lessons that I take from the story include: to follow instructions, to have faith, and to believe that the arrow (approach) will find the deer (success). Extrapolating to the present is to say one must become prepared and believe that she/he has the capacity to provide for self and family. We need to believe in our intrinsic worth and have faith in our abilities to succeed as taught to us through the *choonwensh* principle.

6.7 *Choowaachoots*: Utilizing *Nlakapmux* Vision-Seeking Methods

Choowaachoots speaks to the principle of ascertaining one's purpose in life by being mentored by Grandmothers and family members; training for it; and using ceremonial and spiritual practices. Storytelling, especially from Grandmothers and other family members was closely connected to vision-seeking methods. *Choowaachoots* was experienced as part of 'growing up' in the *Nlakapmux* extended family network, carrying out daily activities through mentorship, and hearing stories all the time. As girls grew up with their Grandmothers, frequent examples were given for when we became "big" girls; task development began with our little berry picking baskets. Grandmothers freely shared their bygone experiences of being little girls and their memories of berry picking, medicine picking, dreaming and visioning. (Verna B, May V.).

Family and community members acknowledged children's developmental phases and they prepared and taught young people their roles and responsibilities, starting from birth. One of the Grandmother interviewees stated that her Grandmother taught her to allow her baby to cry exceptionally loud, never telling her the reason why, however, years later she discovered that this process trained the voice for projection for oratory (Leona L.). This aspect of *Huckpestes* came about when sharing stories of her Grandmother memories.

Since learning was considered a lifelong process, children were always included in family activities; they were not left behind with "baby sitters." It was recognized that they were learning by observing and being a part of the whole family. Children participated in family activities such as plant gathering, gardening, and visiting others. Their self-concept and sense of responsibility were developed through inclusion in family and community life. Ceremonies and storytelling were important means of knowledge transmission within the extended family and community that were carried out enthusiastically. There were many ceremonies and stories to celebrate stages in life and in the community. Ceremonies were a means of sharing wealth and resources. All of the Grandmother interviewees told stories of their coming of age or moontime ceremony.

The Grandmothers felt that they were told of the ancient practices for puberty in order to prepare and support in her cultural pursuit of a vision for a good life for her future family. One's life purpose was often revealed through a vision quest, with spirit helpers from the plant, bird or animal realms. One had to sacrifice such as giving up food and shelter while on a vision quest, therefore, self determination was integral to the practice.

The recognition of our responsibilities for the well-being and strength of self, family and community were realized in each generation through the principle and practices of *choowaachoots*. Young people learned the value of a work ethic in which all work, once started had to be finished and finished well. The Grandmothers played an important mentoring role for their children and grandchildren in order to guide them for their adult roles and responsibilities. One pressing issue that arose during the Grandmothers' group discussion was the disruption in the *Nlakapmux* knowledge of *choowaachoots* due to residential school and assimilationist education.

Some of the Grandmother interviewees acknowledged that they were in the process of learning *choowaachoots*, their life purpose, by learning more about and then sharing ancestral knowledge. In some instances, they were learning with their children because some of these teachings were new to them, which is an unfortunate outcome of colonization. Other Grandmothers indicated they were reviving ancestral customs themselves. Many of the ancestral traditions they had been taught had been dormant for many years and now they felt it was important to teach these customs to their family members.

I asked the Grandmothers about what has changed regarding the transmission of *Nlakapmux* teachings. Most of the Grandmothers acknowledged that much really had changed as "most grandmothers had limited access to their grandchildren now." Few lived with or near their immediate family. This issue of proximity was troubling for the Grandmothers as "families lived apart these days" and living apart was described as an inhibitor from passing on Indigenous Knowledge. Some of the Grandmothers felt that physical distance inhibited communication with grandchildren. Lack of finances often stopped people from visiting relatives living far away. Despite these challenges these Grandmothers are willing to pass down their *Nlakapmux* knowledge.

The Grandmothers also felt optimistic about the future of *Nlakapmux* knowledge transmission. They have noticed a shift in attitude of their adult children, who recognize that Grandmothers have valuable teachings to share.

Another means of knowledge transmission they believe is a challenge and an opportunity for continuing the oral tradition of storytelling involves new electronic technologies. Electronic programs may address digital storytelling; however, the group identified some considerations to think critically about which relate to the structure of the stories and ways to making meaning through stories. For structural considerations, the beginning and middle of the stories may determine their endings or meaning of the story, but conversely, the ending may determine the meaning of the story's beginning and middle. This is *Shinkyap*/Coyote's ways of knowing.

Our *Speta'kl* and *Spilahem* genre of stories represent different time periods. *Speta'kl* refers to historical stories, like creation or origin stories, whereas *Spilahem* emphasize place, personhood, relationships, and kinship with each other, animals/birds, and nature/land stories. In addition, in First Nations storytelling worlds, repetition is a common praxis that facilitates the process of making meaning of the stories (Archibald, 2008).

In *Nlakapmux* oral tradition, we begin to hear stories as a young child and continue to hear and then tell the same stories throughout our lives. We were given the responsibility to make our own meanings from the stories and sometimes we shared the various teachings that we received through a story, although we did not use explicit statements for these purposes. I especially like and appreciate our way of connecting to story teachings in an obtuse manner because this pedagogy makes us as story listeners and learners think for ourselves: there is not one right or wrong answer. This type of story pedagogy conflicts with the pedagogy used in various levels of education today that focus on explicit instruction from learning objectives.

To tell stories, and to make learning connections between past and present, as in *Speta'kl* and *Spilehem* and our transformational stories in educational contexts, would be a welcome change. Storytelling provides one with a crucial way of engaging directly with the contemporary world and is often influenced by the context in which the story is told. This point is reinforced by Julie Cruikshank who learned about the purpose and value of Indigenous stories from Indigenous Elder women (Grandmothers) of the Yukon: "The way a story makes a point or gains its meaning depends on the particular situation it is used to clarify. Like all good stories they contain multiple messages" (Cruikshank, 1990, p. 341). Some of these messages relate to spiritual practices that facilitate healing and wellbeing.

More recently, Judy Iseke, a Metis scholar, (2010) wrote about *The Importance of the Metis Ways of Knowing in Healing Communities*. She collaborated with four Metis Elders originally from Alberta and Saskatchewan: three were Grandfathers and one was a Grandmother. She introduces her Elders' biographies, presents their stories and teachings in their own words, and includes her personal reflections in her work, which I believe to be within the purvue of respectful relationships and presenting research from and in Indigenous voices. The Metis Elders emphasized the important relationship between self and spirit and the role that ceremonies play in creating and sustaining a strong sense of spirituality. The stories and teachings of these four Elders demonstrate their commitment and tenacity to pass on their Indigenous Knowledge, which for them was their life purpose. They persisted despite challenges that they experienced at the community level, which they attribute to colonization. Iseke concludes that the spiritual practices and relationships with the environment "support a good life and help with the healing and wellbeing of people, families, communities, and nations" (p. 2010, p. 94). The spiritual emphasis of the Metis Elders with whom Iseke worked, reminded me of the *Nlakapmux* Grandmothers' teachings about spirituality and how stories can help us with this aspect of our human development.

Today, Grandmothers could revitalize their bedtime and other stories by re-telling these stories in *Nlakapmuxcin.* Stories that were organized in life phases, such as those for children, youth, and adults, and that were told in our language would resemble the traditional pedagogy of hearing and perhaps making meaning with stories. A new recognition that oral tradition can be aided by digital media today is exciting enabling the use of oral tradition anywhere, anytime and anyplace. However, the face-to-face interaction, which creates relationships and synergy between storyteller and listener/learner should never be replaced by digital media. Grandmothers could work with family or community members and culturally sensitive researchers to develop *Spilahem,* current story resources, which reflect the Indigenous approach used by Iseke (2010). We, the Nlakapmux Grandmothers, could live up to our responsibilities and demonstrate our teaching roles and responsibilities for children, parents, families and communities in this way. It is time to reclaim our place and space demonstrating leadership in intergenerational and storytelling pedagogy.

Indeed the challenge is for *Nlakapmux* tribal people today to live the *Nlakapmux* ways as my pedagogical principles outline concepts and behaviours/practices for living a good life. Through the process of *conscientization Nlakapmux* families may consciously examine, decide upon what traditional parts of their tribalism to keep, and then make a concerted effort, developing a plan to accomplish that. To do less is tokenism.

6.8 *Nmeenlth Coynchoots*: Incorporating *Nlakapmux* Knowledge

The Grandmother interviewees and my memories of the teachings that we received in childhood were embedded in our physical, spiritual, emotional, and mental realms through our learning relationships with our Grandmothers. They had a story for each of the learnings we required in life's journey such as expectations and responsibilities for living a healthy life, caring for family and others, being generous and sharing our resources, and passing on these learnings to children and others.

It is these stories that we are sharing, using *peteenuushem* reflections, the last concept to be shared in the emerging Nlakapmux principles as defined by this research effort. *Peteenuushem* contextualizes the *Nmeenlth coynchoots*. The following examples from my memory stories demonstrate the intergenerational learning that I experienced with my Grandmothers and then I share stories of how this learning is carried out between my daughter Yvonne and her grandson.

I remember my Grandmother, *Tiilaa,* teaching me how to behave in the store when we went shopping together. She would keep me close to her, speaking gently, telling me the object that she wanted to buy. I would then tell the storekeeper\owner. *Tiilaa* taught me how to hoe the garden, sweep the floor, feed the chickens, collect eggs, pick berries, make yeast bread and bake apple pie, all before I was seven years old. I related this story numerous times to my children and their cousins. My daughter, who is a Grandmother, taught her ten-year-old grandson to clean, vacuum, mop the floor, cook breakfast, and make sandwiches for lunch. He also learned to make both tea and coffee for his grandmother *(Yvonne S).*

My Grandmother *Tiilaa* attended my first concert at my public school when I turned seven, travelling the one-hour train ride to do so. My great-Grandmother, *Lamiinak,* showed me how to make lunches for the workers in the field, how to make our *shoohooshum*\soapberry dessert with a cedar whisk in a cedar basket. She also taught me how to pray for our health, safe travel and rain. She showed me that I had to be home a certain time if I was wanting to stay with her and also to wear proper clothing, modest clothing, even covering a bathing suit for our mile walk until we arrived at the swimming place. This story has been shared with grandchildren when they visit me.

Nana (Yvonne S.) in raising her grandson, attends his Christmas concert and parent-teacher meetings, takes him for walks to the beach, and teaches him appropriate behavior such as refraining from fights and quarrelling. She encourages him to be kind to others, and not to "sass" adults. Nana and grandson smudge and pray together. She also teaches him about Indian plant medicines and ways to protect the body, mind and spirit by using the eagle feather (Yvonne S).

Grandmother *Tiilaa* taught me to share what I had, if I got a duplicate of something, however small, I had to share it with my siblings or even a complete stranger. One time I got two dolls at Christmas. I was told I had to give one away. Much to my dismay then, however, now I realize it was a teaching of sharing and generosity.

Yvonne S (Nana) is teaching her grandson to share games with her and his uncle. *Nana* gives money to her grandson when walking down the street to give it to someone who has his or her hat out. There is a gender difference here because Nana is a single Grandmother, teaching her grandson; ordinarily the

Grandpa would be sharing teachings with the grandson. However, she is teaching generosity, which is appropriate for both genders, in my view.

I recall at celebrations, we as children sat quietly, observing the speeches and moved only when told by our Grandmothers. *Nana (Yvonne S.)* tells her grandson how to behave at current cultural events. She feels strongly that when children learn these protocols the family and community benefits because a standard of behavior is expected.

In remembering great-granny, Alice, encouraging me to read stories and her mail to her, I felt a certain importance. I was responsible for reading Grandmother *Tiilaa's* mail after Grandfather died, when I was fourteen. Then she also asked me to accompany her to the bank as her interpreter. The skills I gained in this process familiarized me with the formality of having money i*n the bank. Nana (Yvonne S)* and her grandson go to the bank together and Nana has helped him open a bank account. They share problem-solving a word, spelling and homework on the computer. *Nana* and her grandson read stories together and watch movies together.

In reflecting on the acts of growing up in my family where I was the first to learn English, I was needed to transact English on behalf of us all. I became the shopping assistant, the translator for letters, the letter writer and book reader for my Grandmothers. Consequently I grew up with a feeling of importance and confidence.

Returning to others in our *Nlakapmux* community, Shirley Sterling (1997) in her doctoral thesis titled *The Grandmother Stories: Oral Tradition and the Transmission of Culture*, shares her *Nlakapmux* knowledge that she received from her Grandmother, *Yetco.* Shirley recounted a dream where *Yetco* came to help her with an assignment and her subsequent realization that she could write about her Grandmother as an example of someone who lived the *Nlakapmux* concept of respect (p. 137). Shirley's reflections exemplify the *Nlakapmux* concept of *peteenuushem,* the next principle to be discussed. Shirley's scholarship has important implications for kindergarten to grade 12 education. Because the foundation had been set for her and young girls through dream sharing, our Grandmothers can return to this practice when needed or when we are ready.

6.9 *Peteenuushem*: Reflecting on Learning and Relearning Lifelong Lessons

The wholistic approach to education requires much creativity and imagination to address the learning gaps in our education today. It is incumbent on us Grandmothers, parents and educators to *peteenuushem-thinking* a way out of this malaise. An in-depth review of our *Nlakapmux peteenuushem,* reflection and our emergent *Nlakapmux* principles, pedagogies and praxes must be made.

In the *Caustem* of these principles today, some attention and effort may be necessary in order to decolonize or unlearn self-limiting behaviours brought about by colonization attempts. There are ways to reclaim our heritage, but in so doing it may be necessary for a consistent program of *consciencitization* (Freire, 2004) and transformation. Generally speaking and at the risk of digression, we the *Nlakapmux people,* based on the historic abuses and colonization by the Throne and Altar, need a period of time for unlearning to address these destructive tendencies. Therefore, incorporating *Nlakapmux* epistemology would probably appear to be impossible or irrelevant to some community members, however, in some cases, a deliberate move toward cultural revival may suffice. In other cases, a complete healing program and re-education must occur, which could be part of a decolonizing process as noted by Lanai &

Burgess: "...an outline of the process of decolonization... [includes] the following elements: a) rediscovery and recovery; b) mourning; c) dreaming; d) commitment; and e) action" (2000, p.152).

The first phase of rediscovery and recovery is a suggested foundation for decolonization. In this phase, culture, language, identity are rediscovered or reclaimed and are the basis from which to continue with healing; these factors guide the actions to follow. Mourning is the second phase where the state of victimization is realized and understood and grieving losses occurs. Often, anger and resentment towards the oppressor surfaces. Perhaps an immersion in the history of colonization occurs as one learns the magnitude of cultural loss. The third phase, our dreaming, is characterized as being crucial. Dreams or visions of a new reality form the foundation for the subsequent actions. A recent work entitled "Expanding Knowledge through Dreaming, Wampum and Visual Arts" by Dawn Marsden states:

> To validate dreaming as a research tool, we must remember that dreaming is symbolically where we process, synthesise and resolve information, question experiences we have each day, with the understanding, we have accrued so far, to produce understanding 'new to us.' Some dreams or which we may call visions or gifts are especially helpful in answering our questions, guiding our actions, or making sense of our world (2004, p.7).

In our *Nlakapmux* way, *peteenuushem* must not be rushed, as it requires much reflection, repetition and introspection. Rushing this process may produce short-sighted goals and create conflict among people involved in the process.

The next phase, commitment, entails that the group is unified and strong. There is a firm commitment to and consensus for change, which the group envisions. The final phase is characterized by action and by implementing the commitment. My final comments on this process note that decolonization is not a linear process nor is it ever complete and that individuals or groups may revisit different phases throughout their lifespan. Sometimes we may go into a limbotic state. When one experiences the condition of 'limbo' we can assume we are 'stuck', therefore, we need to seek support to move on. Linda Tuhiwai Smith suggests, "Coming to know the past has been a part of the critical pedagogy of decolonization" (2004, p. 34).

In *Nlakapmuxcin,* then, *huckpeshtes* (discovering or finding out what happened to us) helps us decolonize. In addition, Smith also emphasises the process of decolonization includes the actions of recovering Indigenous stories and history, and retelling them through an Indigenous pedagogy. Likewise, I recommend recovering our *Shinkyap*/Coyote teachings. Smith elaborates on this process of self-determination and suggests that it includes a cyclical process of decolonization, healing, transformation and mobilization (2004, p. 116).

These ideas resonate with those of Paulo Freire (2009) in *Pedagogy of Hope*: to acquire freedom in the decolonized and delineated order, the colonized must break their silence and struggle to retake possession of their humanity and identity He defines oppression as dehumanization. He further asserts that in order for the oppressed to escape this dehumanization (defined as the loss of humanity), the oppressed must engage in a process of humanization or becoming "more fully human" (ibid, p. 44).

Humanization occurs when liberation from the oppressor begins. Freire states that the oppressed must reframe their worlds from being hopeless to being ones that can be completely changed and liberated; this includes freedom for the oppressed and the oppressors. This process requires *conscientization*, which requires leadership and critical reflection of and by the oppressed. The solutions must come from within the community as demonstrated by my own learning (as an insider) and lessons that I have taken from a dream I had about my childhood relatives. I will share this story with you now.

Recently this year I dreamed of my three girl cousins, who were women singers. When they were children they attended Residential School and when they came home in the summer, they visited us frequently. They died in early motherhood and in my dream, Shirley was singing a hymn and Evelyn the older sister was crying, so I asked her why she was crying? In response, she replied she wanted to sing her Grandmother's song, not the church hymn they were forced to sing.

In my dream I told her to go ahead and sing her Grandmother's song, which she did happily. I was relieved to learn that she still had the ability to choose her song spiritually and did so. My analysis and reflection showed me the power of transformation resides in us in our sleep. In my cousin's reclamation of her spiritual song I was able to claim mine too. I realized that the choice is mine to sing or not to sing my traditional song.

Here comes the challenging part, as in my deepest reflection I can see the erosion of our ways through to my great grandson. Indeed we are four generations now and live vastly different daily lives than we lived when I was a child. Tradition and protocols are almost non-existent, and with an absence of community activities, there is a kind of limbo pervading modern *Nlakapmux* life. Just as in my cedar root basket-making metaphor, creativity and improvisation is called for to weave the strands of old and new teachings together to address the disparity in how we fulfil our obligations within a family, often more questions than answers arise. However, all the Grandmothers believe that we must call on our ancestral traditions to support one another during this time of transition from traditional to modern living *Nlakapmux* ways of being.

6.10 Summary

The findings of my research on an *emerging Nlakapmux Developing Wisdom Theory* assists in the expansion, connection, and validation of our Indigenous personal, family, and community wisdom and success in living a good life. In seeking a balance between traditional *Nlakapmux* and mainstream knowledge, recognition of the need to be bi/multi -cultural in today's world (being able to walk in two or more worlds) are important options for today's *Nlakapmux* people.

This idea of knowing and using traditional and current ideas is mentioned in an article written by Indigenous scholar Yvonne McLeod, in the *Canadian Journal of Native Education (2003).* She suggests that "NITEP [Native Indian Teacher Education Program] students need to learn the leadership style where one is able to 'walk in two worlds-hand and hand-hands back and hands forward!" (McLeod, 2003, p.111). I, too, believe there is an opportunity for educational processes to be designed by Aboriginal communities, that would deliver the necessary knowledge, skills and attitudes that could address present community needs by building upon traditional Indigenous ways of knowing.

Blending of our Indigenous traditional teachings and other Indigenous teachings may be a way to move our learning and teaching agendas further toward Indigenous success. Therefore, in the educational process today, our ability to trust and share our traditional principles, concepts, philosophies, epistemologies, pedagogies and praxes are recommended.

A review of the distinctive *Nlakapmux* pedagogy and praxis of the *Nlakapmuxcin* may be summed up in many ways, the following are some examples.

> Preserving and conserving Mother Nature was one. The other would be to be self-sufficient and the other would be the connection to the extended family. You know it doesn't matter like Grandmother would always say, don't ever be bad to anybody because you don't know if you're related to them. You be careful, check out who you're related to in case you ever date your cousin you know. So the importance of knowing

> your identity and who your family is was a big thing too. I tell that to my children be careful. You ask me the name of that boy if you want to go out with him first. In that way I think, well that's good because there has been a time when we may have lost track of someone. Because our families have gotten so large and so spaced out that we don't know where our family is (Leona L. Interview, 2010).

Many of the Grandmothers interviewed say we should follow the practices of living in ceremony, being prayerful, grateful for the past and present and expectant of the future; this practice puts us in the here and now - *chaachaawoowh* experiences leading up to wisdom facilitates h*uckpestes*, a concept that explains that one is acquiring/discovering learning and therefore growing to wisdom.

A common theme of knowledge transmission occurring in the intact *Nlakapmux f*amily was freely demonstrated to the child at the appropriate time, without explanation, but by accompanying their Grandmothers in daily activities. Children's questions were answered; however, the teachings were often indirect through storytelling and experiential activities such as food gathering, preparing food and medicine plants - *Choowaachoots t*he Grandmothers stressed the importance of developing and maintaining a welcoming, loving home environment that provided safety for the developing child.

Loving the children and teaching by storytelling were a part of everyday living. This is exemplified in my recollections of stories, of early childhood experiences, including those of all members of the family and of the role of the significant Grandmothers, playing their parts in teaching me about life and appropriate behaviors. These are techniques and methods that have and continue to inform my own teachings and interactions with my grandchildren.

In summary, the whole issue of relationship between teacher and learner has been emphasized and illumined. In fact a positive relationship, *Takemshooknooqua is* inherent in the *Nlakapmux* principles. This relationship of being connected promotes teachers' ability to relate and inter-relate learnings and conversely teachings to others. *Takemshooknooqua* relationships, allow for the building, collection and collaboration of teachings among wisdom holders and learners. The *Nlakapmux* language as a form of conversation for the family must be included.

The whole hypothesis for current teachers to include language as complements to all classes must become a reality. A new recognition that oral tradition can be aided by digital technology today is exciting and challenging. Oral tradition may now be used anywhere, anytime and anyplace. We, the grandmothers with

Nlakapmux wisdom live up to our responsibilities and demonstrate our ancestral roles and responsibilities for parents, families and communities. It is time to reclaim our place and space demonstrating leadership in intergenerational storytelling *Nlakapmux* teaching and learnings in our current day *Spilahem*.

Chapter Seven: *Waasheet*: Beginning a New Journey

This final chapter presents my "voice" and "consciousness" along with the understandings that I gleaned from *Nlakapmux* Grandmothers and others. It also reviews the findings for the study's goals, the significance and contribution of the research, its strengths and limitations, its potential applications, and gives suggestions for future research directions drawing on the research knowledge gained from *Nlakapmux* Grandmothers' stories and their pedagogies. I close this chapter with my personal reflections on carrying out the *Nlakapmux Developing Wisdom Theory* and I share one new *Speta'kl.*

7.1 *Nlakapmux*: Developing Wisdom Theory (NDWT)

I created or wove a NDWT based on a thorough review and reflective process of my life story through storywork, a wholistic and traditional *Nlakapmux* analysis of 11 *Nlakapmux* Grandmother interviews and circle talks, and a critical review of historical literature written by early ethnographers and anthropologists and literature by *Nlakapmux* scholars. My methodology evolved into an *Nlakapmux Grandmother's Methodology* that used the aforementioned research approaches in response to the following major research questions.

- How did Grandmothers pass on *Nlakapmux* knowledge (values, beliefs, and teachings) and pedagogy?
- What were important teachings and pedagogies?
- How did *Nlakapmux* intergenerational learning, oral tradition, and teachings contribute to living a good life?
- Which *Nlakapmux* teachings and pedagogies are practiced in the Grandmothers' families today?
- What are the challenges and opportunities for continuing these *Nlakapmux* teachings and pedagogies in family and community settings?

The findings of these questions revealed eight *Nlakapmux* principles that comprise the *Nlakapmux Developing Wisdom Theory.* To obtain *Nlakapmux authenticity*, I chose to utilize the *Nlakapmuxcin* language to conceptualize and describe the eight epistemological principles for our pedagogy (teachings) and praxis (learnings). They were then translated into the English language. From the perspectives of *Nlakapmux* Grandmothers The principles are as follows. However they are not in order of priority.

- *Takemshooknooqua*, Knowing we are connected: land, animals, plants and people;

- *ChaaChawoowh*, Celebrating people and land joyously;
- *Huckpestes*, Developing lifelong learning and wisdom;
- *Huztowaahh,* Giving lovingly to family and community;
- *Choownensh*, Succeeding in endeavours;
- *Choowaachoots*, Utilizing *Nlakapmux* vision-seeking methods;
- *Nmeenlth coynchoots*, Incorporating *Nlakapmux* knowledge; and
- *Peteenushem*, Reflecting on learning and relearning lifelong lessons.

Even though the NDWT defines teachings and learnings that were practiced in our ancestral societies, it can also inform teachings and learnings in current and future *Nlakapmux* family, extended family, and community. In Chapter Six, I presented the traditional meaning of each principle and gave Grandmothers' examples of past and current practice where applicable. I also suggested ways that some of the principles could be used in current family and educational settings. The analysis and findings of Chapters Four, Five and Six also integrated applicable literature/research in the area of my research.

The principles or concepts t*akemshooknooqua, chaachawoowh, huckpestes,* huztowaahh *choonwensh*, *choowaachoots*, *nmeenlth coynchoots, and peteenuushem* broadly outline the manner in which *Nlakapmux* people, especially Grandmothers, see their world and how these help one live a good life. The Grandmothers and I discussed the traditional form of their Grandmothers' work that involved making a cedar root basket during the group circle dialogue. They encouraged me to use cedar root basket making as a metaphor to refine and apply the understandings that emerged during the wholistic analysis of their interview/talks.

7.2 Implications for Application of the Research

The emergent principles of the *Nlakapmux Developing Wisdom Theory* require more development and application in the learning and teaching processes of *Nlakapmux* individuals. The circle talks were a wonderful way to bring together Indigenous Grandmothers who had common cultural backgrounds. We talked and told stories about what and how we learned from our Grandmothers' and other family members' pedagogies. We built upon each other's ideas and re-awakened our memories about some forms of knowledge that we had either temporarily forgotten or had not quite understood some of the teachings that we received. I suggest that this form of discussion and interaction could be replicated by other *Nlakapmux* families where Grandmothers or various family members get together to talk about their traditional forms of learning or where they could use the *Nlakapmux Developing Wisdom Theory* as a catalyst for dialogue. *Nlakapmux* community groups might sponsor such sessions that are at first family-based, then families could share their results to create a wider community perspective.

Educators, especially those with public and Band schools in the Merritt area and the Nicola Valley Institute of Technology, which is an Aboriginal post-secondary institution, could incorporate the results of the study to improve the delivery of knowledge transmission for *Nlakapmux* and other learners. They could meet with *Nlakapmux* Grandmothers to discuss the *Nlakapmux Developing Wisdom Theory* and discuss how they could develop classroom pedagogies based on the principles.

Although some identification and similarities have been made to the *Okanagan and Secwepmec* First Nations, who are also of the Interior Salish tribes, I have focused on the *Nlakapmux*. Based on these findings educators in those areas may need to learn culturally appropriate methods of instruction for Indigenous learners or discover common approaches such as storytelling that give learners flexibility in learning from stories.

7.3 Significance and Contribution of the Research

The results of this study add to the research pertaining to the facilitation of learning and teaching success for *Nlakapmux* people. Scholars such as Shirley Sterling (1992, 1997), Annie York (1993) and Darwin Hanna and Mamie Henry (1995) have published their thoughts on *Nlakapmux* philosophies, stories, and life ways. Sterling's work focuses on her Grandmother's educational philosophies and traditional practices, which has some similarity to my research. My new contribution to *Nlakapmux* knowledge and scholarship is the development of a theory of pedagogy and learning based on Grandmothers' traditional teachings and my understandings gained through the process of undertaking this research. My work uses the *Nlakapmuxcin* language to frame the principles that comprise this theory, which is also a new contribution to scholarship in this area. Other works may discuss the *Nlakapmuxcin* language but they don't use it as the conceptual base for their scholarship.

This study also contributes to Indigenous scholarship about wholistic learning and wholistic methodological analysis by using a culturally specific example. I show that a common conceptual model of the Plains Medicine Wheel can be used to understand *Nlakapmux* good life physical, emotional, intellectual, and spiritual teachings and that it can work in concert with a traditional form of

Nlakapmux Knowledge: cedar root basket making. Through this research process of weaving together various forms of knowledges, I also developed a new *Nlakapmux approach:* Grandmother's Methodology, in order to practice respectful, responsible, reverent, and reciprocal actions to the people with whom I worked on this research project (Archibald, 2008; Kirkness & Barnhardt, 1991).

7.3 Strengths and Limitations of the Research

The strengths and limitations of the study focus on methodological matters. Sometimes, an example could be both a limitation and strength, which will be pointed out where applicable. Although the interviewees were few in number (N=11) and the sampling was restricted to seven of my relatives (mainly siblings) and four other *Nlakapmux* community members; the data gained was rich in pedagogical principles and practices. The exemplary quality of knowledge shared is the strength of my research; therefore, I do not consider the small participant numbers a limitation.

At first, the individual interviews did not proceed smoothly when I used the interview guide. The older Grandmothers did not seem to address the interview questions. They spoke about topics that they felt were pertinent such as kinship and family history. The interviews were up to three hours and once we became comfortable with the process, the time went by too quickly. I felt that the questions and the time limit of the interviews limited the scope and depth of what Grandmothers shared.

The strengths of the research also relate to methodology. The Grandmother participants are named with their permission. Their biographical information is presented as they wished. Their individual contributions are attributed to and owned by them in order to give them credit and recognition and to demonstrate respect and honour to their *Nlakapmux* families. The Grandmother's story information/data was solely interpreted by me before I presented the findings to the group for their reaction.

Because this was Indigenous research by an insider of the culture/community that was the focus of the study, it could be called a huge limitation, due to bias; however, it could also be viewed as a huge advantage. My ability to speak the insider language gave me access to new data as participants spoke about some concepts only in the Indigenous language and not in English. My ability to ask for clarification in the *Nlakapmuxcin* language was especially helpful. Finally, the categories emerging for the *Nlakapmux* principles were interpreted at first by only me as a fluent *Nlakapmuxcin* speaker and reviewed by circle talk (focus group). The distinction between pedagogy and praxis was also my responsibility and honour.

7.4 Implications for Future Research

Further research about the proposed principles for the *Nlakapmux Developing Wisdom Theory* and other possible factors that may contribute to the development of *Nlakapmux* wisdom is necessary. Researching each principle's application singly or in concert with other principles is recommended. I undertook a wholistic approach for the development of my proposed theory to reflect the nature of *Nlakakpmux* epistemology as I have lived and understood it and how the Grandmother participants also talked about it.

Another area for research involves understanding the pedagogic or practice/praxis components of the principles. At first, I began to identify the principles as either pedagogy or praxis. For example, the following five principles seemed oriented more for praxis, or practice/application of what is learned; *huztoowah, chaachawoowh, choowaachoots, nmeemlth coynchoots, and peteenushem.* However, they also could be forms of pedagogy or teaching. Further refinement of the nature of these principles and how they can be transformed into current day pedagogy and praxis would benefit from further research.

This research opens up debate over the differences and similarities in ways and means to learning, teaching, and the development of wisdom for *Nlakapmux* people. It also appears that learning and teaching were and are connected to rites of passage historically, for example the puberty rites, so one may introduce teachings and learnings for current day life passages to develop a new educational approach among *Nlakapmux* people. Teachings that are age and context appropriate may be of significance for further research. Some rites of life passage could be revitalized within a specific family context, while others could be undertaken at community, school, or post-secondary contexts.

One other area for research could focus on Grandfathers' traditional roles and their forms of knowledge and pedagogy. I chose to focus on Grandmothers and excluded Grandfathers from the interviews and circle talks. I am aware that this exclusion could be considered a limitation of my research but I also felt it was important to start with only Grandmothers' knowledge and pedagogy in order to get a gendered understanding of their perspectives. Grandfathers could be asked to share their stories and perspectives using the same topics as Grandmothers in order to compare their respective responses; perhaps adding new theoretical dimensions to the NDWT. Further discussion and research needs to be done regarding Indigenous Intellectual Property Rights and Indigenous stories.

I share my final research reflections in next section, as an *Nlakapmux* Grandmother and scholar about the results of my research and language challenges. I also return to the theoretical ideas of double-voice and double-consciousness and discuss implications for my professional and leadership practice.

7.5 Personal Reflections from a Nlakapmux Grandmother and Scholar

The goal of building and maintaining culturally sustainable Indigenous communities has become more critical in the 21st century. Our younger generations of Indigenous people now significantly outnumber the adult and Elder generations (Canada Census, 2006). A new vision is needed to develop responsive approaches to Indigenous Knowledge transmission suitable to sustain us. It is time for drastic review and change and for developing a collective vision. I took responsibility to look for new ways or a new vision to carry out traditional or 'old' forms of *Nlakapmux*/Indigenous knowledge because I felt that this type of knowledge has sustained my ancestors and their communities for years.

In my personal process of developing and acquiring wisdom as an *Nlakapmuxcin* speaking grandmother, I engaged in a process of recollection, reflection and examination of previous life activities, questions and epiphanies. My academic journey began in earnest in the 1980's following a progression of events that reconnected me to my emotional and spiritual psyche. Through the process of researching and writing my thesis of *Nlakapmux* Grandmother stories, I employed the *Nlakapmux* epistemologies present in my *Nlakapmux* world: the *Nlakapmuxcin* language, the extended family, *Spilahem* and *Speta'kl* stories, wholistic teachings for living a good life, and the traditional cedar root basket-making work of Grandmothers.

My resolve to strengthen, share and express in thesis format more salient points of our traditional forms of pedagogy and praxis has taken a concerted effort with many challenges. One prominent challenge was documenting orally told and remembered *Nlakapmux* epistemology, then identifying pertinent *Nlakapmuxcin* concepts, and finally translating them into the English language. My challenge with documenting a written form of the *Nlakapmuxcin* language included the use of phonetic spelling that I developed for it. Those who know the language should be able to sound it out. When I speak this language orally, there is no confusion about its orality; there aren't different "speaking" systems.

In these personal reflections, I would be remiss if I did not address the theoretical issue of double-voice and double-consciousness (Stigter, 2008). In Chapter Four, I analyzed historical and contemporary literature/scholarship about *Nlakapmux* people from outsider and insider perspectives. The historical scholarship presents us from the eyes and consciousness of others/outsiders. Because archival documentation is all that some people may have access to, if they are not fortunate to have family or community members with traditional knowledge, then they may look at themselves "through the eyes of others" (double vision that includes themselves but not really seeing or understanding their own Indigenous standpoint). Through the development of my dissertation I believe I have gained an ability to describe and discuss this phenomenon.

I followed the pathway of other contemporary Indigenous scholars to experience another meaning of double-consciousness in which we critique the historical and outsider representations of Indigenous people and learn from Indigenous insiders so that we can look at ourselves predominantly through our own eyes and consciousness as well as other representations. I also experienced double-voice and double-consciousness through the bi-lingual approach that I used for this thesis.

I learned to appreciate and use the forms of the *Speta'kl* and *Spilahem* stories that have ceremonial and conversational forms, which reflect the concept of double-voice. The struggle to express myself in both languages, and understanding the conceptual differences that are inherent in these languages were constant tensions, which could be an example of double-voice and double-consciousness. For me, the process of writing this thesis from my *Nlakapmuxcin* roots has aligned my voice and my consciousness to help me continue on the journey to wholeness and to living a good life.

An expectation and outcome of my Educational Doctorate thesis is that it has application to my professional leadership practice. My professional work as a social worker in the First Nations Addictions counselling field will benefit further from my documentation of our *Nlakapmux* traditional knowledge. I now have a stronger understanding of the dynamics and benefit to wholistic Indigenous learning and development. There is much relevance in the reconnection of Indigenous mind and spirit as a path to enjoy wholeness for those seeking solutions to current personal and family, social, cultural, mental, and emotional issues.

In my roles as Instructor and Elder, I can continue to relate these ancestral conceptual ways of knowing to lead a good life for our community to my students. I can encourage and challenge those whom I teach and mentor to learn more about their families and Grandmothers' ways of knowing and teaching. Helping others recognize the resilience and strength of *Nlakapmux* ancestors and ourselves can be done by sharing my thesis with others to gain this insight. In the pursuit of this dissertation, presenting my emerging Grandmother's wisdom development theory, in its embryonic form has been rewarding for me.

Storytelling as a means of sharing and understanding Indigenous knowledge has many contextual venues. Sharing and analyzing my story of my becoming an "Elder" and experiencing *huckpeshtes* about this coming of age role, to be an "Elder" within a family, extended family and tribe is a life long process and may be considered wisdom learning. In my analysis, reflecting on life events and learning from these experiences has lead to the development of wisdom and contributes to becoming a wise Elder. As an Elder I apply my learnings from the teachings from the *Kulthkulthmeen* 'old ones/wisdom keepers. The key to clarifying these teachings lies in privileging our Indigenous voice, thus producing the valuable interpretations which inform others of the role of First Nations 'Elder' traditionally and in today's modern world. Conscientization of the developing Elder may enable them to take their rightful roles in our societies.

We, the Indigenous Grandmothers, family and community members will face many barriers as we revitalize traditional forms of family pedagogy and transform them into current day practice. However, we can begin small and grow, find allies and coalitions, perhaps, with other adjacent communities, or other Indigenous peoples in the world. It will be a challenge to create, maintain, defend, extend and preserve our right to completeness of each and every person to live a good life. We must develop a cultural literacy connecting the head, heart, spirit and hands to lay a common foundation to work from the ground up, expressing relationship with self, family, clan, tribe, locale, continents, and cosmos to become complete, whole and fully human. This is the *shnaam*/prayer and hope of my research!

7.6 Conclusion

My research interest about *Nlakapmux* Grandmothers within our tribal context is a culmination of a lifetime interest. I utilized a critical reflective style of analysis stemming from my awareness and learnings as an *Nlakapmux* child, youth, mother and Grandmother. Through interviewing, documenting and reflecting on these processes throughout the development of this thesis, I developed eight *Nlakapmux* principles pertaining to basic tenets of *Nlakapmux* Grandmothers' pedagogies and praxes. My writings challenge the prevalent Western ideologies, contest hegemonies, unmask power inequities and reclaim the validity of *Nlakapmux* perspectives.

What I have gleaned, learned and relearned will continue to find cultural expression in the lessons and teachings that I share as an Elder. I found it exciting to seek from within our own culture, a culture that has sustained us since time immemorial. Whether we call on action research, engender dialogue, and tap blood memories (Holmes, 2000) through dreams and visions, with the collective in mind we will continue in the growth and completeness of all members of *Nlakapmux* society, transforming to one of enlightenment, joy and being in the highest thought. A people who are at this place in time will be able to share great things required for the teachings and lessons not only for the tribe but also for humanity, as we are interdependent with our neighbours, nature and the ecology.

The *Nlakapmux* Grandmothers' intergenerational methods of Indigenous knowledge transmission, provides a framework for *Nlakapmux* and Indigenous families that want to document and better understand the processes of intergenerational pedagology. This is essential, as today, many of us appear to be preoccupied with consumer conduct. I believe our present difficulties are exacerbated by our loss of fluency in our Mother tongue. Highlighting family oriented teaching styles/methods and practices in *Nlakapmuxcin*, as I have done in my thesis, bring these elements out of their present obscurity. Through personal reflection in particular, I argue that Grandmothers' teaching methodology is deliberate and strategic, especially in how and what information is transmitted. I believe this thesis captures historical facts and influences, as well as individual and family growth and development based on *Nlakapmux* Knowledge. The essence of my life story illuminates how traditional wholistic values may facilitate success for *Nlakapmux* people today. I claim my right, as an *Nlakapmux* grandmother, to my story and subsequent learning's and teachings, thus asserting my intellectual sovereignty as an *Nlakapmux* person. I end my thesis with a new *Speta'kl* story that I have created and which incorporates the principles of the *Nlakapmux Developing Wisdom Theory: Beaver Teachings*. It is presented in both *Nlakapmuxcin* and English languages (see Table 2 below).

Table 2: My *Spilahem Beaver Teachings*

Nlakapmuxcin	English
Le peyaoosh, woit ha-a skeehasaa lluquoopa.	Once long ago, while Mother Beaver
Kwielt towas eekquilah has tlookmeens a tehaanuus chootas a cheethaws	was sleeping and then awakens from a dream wondering if she could remember to build a house
Meemeechuck alth coynchoots alth chaawaash	The Beaver couple sit together and discuss
tehanoose wheesh chooteehush ,	what is important to teach the children,
Chaawiit meechoqu ash quenchootmsh alth quoinchootmth ash taawoosh weeh choonamash a shmats	how it should be taught and talked about why it must be taught to their children
Tehanoosh weea shahchoos. Chooweet l heenoosh Wheet a kinshaquatenmash ash chooeetsh whe haaa weeatim axe shawaatem wheehaa canoehateesh alth choonamateesh.	They discussed how long ago, there was a community of beavers who lived in one end of the lake and they wanted to reconnect with any one from that place to help them as they were young inexperienced beavers and had forgotten how to do these teachings.
Ash kwoicheeaa weeahash kulthmeen. Chaachaawh ah nguishathkins ash lalahanshtem. Chooteehish al achoosh ash shaawatem cantem chooit alth weekt peteenoshem Choot leshkiwuh	They journeyed to the other end of the lake to visit their neighbours, and there, they were welcomed to lunch, where the entire family was enjoying lunch, they spoke of their needs they said "well, let's think back to how you were taught!"
Looqumeenaah, nashchemsh lhen skeeza althen skatsaa le chooteeheesh chitxht Yameet ahwoolth shyaap	So, Mr. Beaver went first and he thought and thought and said, "I

sheecheesse alth kakatch akas cansh axe chootsash a cheethash alth choot alth sheeza Lukmeenalthchoo alth skeeza a choot nahanoosh a intukcheenten Ash bantsh a skatsa alth skeezaa weeahim tish yeahh tuks shyap yameet alth chooeet kukstyap Huckpestes alth skatzaalth skeeza looqumeens a choonamaash. a shmayts choochoots Chaachaawuh takemsnooqua chookoos lapnough yeaa tuks peteenooshem. *Chooowoo alth whistoosh a tehanoosh weesh schoos Yea-a alth ash hooaks ash eekwelwh a tsehoosh chootesh a schoosh* *Kueelt ash nushch yamee Tlak a shukas ash lukmeensh skeeza ahaa shwensch nkishyatkens a weekem ta nhaneeten as luggtash a shoopash ash schoowups chachawuh alth weeh choonamash a shmayts alth tsoise ush yameet ash chooeets nahum yeaah a choonwansh a nlakatens a nguesaatkens ash taawoosh weeh choonamash a shmayts Tehanoosh weea* **Nlakapmuxcin**	remember my mother and father taking me along when they were building our house, they gave offerings to the tree brothers and sisters who would sacrifice themselves for the house" and then Mrs. Beaver chimed in and said; "I remember how it was Mother beaver who showed where the entry ways were to be positioned and then Father and Mother went to find the appropriate trees and gave offerings and thanks for the gifts of the trees." So, within the company of their neighbours Mr. and Mrs. Beaver remembered how to teach their young, house building, food-gathering and child rearing. The neighbours welcomed them and said to them "do not forget harmony and balance." So on their way home across the lake they talked of how they would work in fun and community visits to their neighbours on a regular basis. The beaver pair thought and vowed to dream again that night for direction to complete their task. **English**
shahchoos Chooweet l heenoosh Wheet a kinshaquatenmash ash chooeetsh whe haaa weeatim axe shawaatem wheehaa canoehateesh alth choonamateesh *Ash kwoicheeaa weeahash kulthmeen Chaachaawh ah nguishathkins ash lalahanshtem Chooteehish al achoosh ash shaawatem cantem chooit alth*	They awakened with the rising of the sun, and remembered the prayer ceremonies they used to do at sunrise and then Mrs. Beaver remembered that the adults used to provide protection, remembering the slapping noise of their parents tails to warn of danger being nearby. They were now very excited to teach their young and at

weekt peteenoshem Choot leshkiwuh Looqumeenaah, nashchemsh lhen skeeza althen skatsaa le chooteeheesh chitxht Yameet ahwoolth shyaap sheecheesse alth kakatch akas cansh axe chootsash a cheethash alth choot alth sheeza *Lukmeenalthchoo alth skeeza a choot nahanoosh a intukcheenten Ash bantsh a skatsa alth skeezaa weeahim tish yeahh tuks shyap yameet alth chooeet kukstyap*	sundown they offered prayers of thanksgiving for all the lessons of sustenance and protection and guidance of their beaver community especially what is important to teach the children; how it should be taught; and of course they talked about why it must be taught.

We, *Nlakapmux,* could take a lesson from the Beavers and go to our community and ask the *Kulthmeen* (wisdom keepers) how to develop this teaching/learning to help the people today to discover their purpose and learn the things they need to learn to be complete, therefore finding meaning in how to live a good life; how to pray and ask for help, and dream and vision for the guidance of what to pass along to help the community members succeed in life. The Elders/wisdom keepers in my area know the teachings offered by water and rose bush; the elements will be given offerings and consulted at daybreak and at sunset for four days, to call on the teachings of the four directions. At this time we focus on deep thoughts about travels and experiences, how they worked or did not work, what may have been missing, what will be considered and reflected upon;

from this new re- thinking a deeper inspiration, desire and motivation will spring, which is the (house) making/ready stage.

Next all will be ready to engage in the creative process, incorporating a wholistic framework based on experience, observation, making an outline of the lessons, always flexible/subject to change and to take the appropriate time to execute the lesson, allowing for time for each member to give observations, comments and questions in a safe environment free from threat and fears. At this time all elaborate on our visions by including others into the dialogue to enrich our visions, remembering the extended family concept and "it takes a community to raise a child." Space is then created and a time is given to develop a collective vision in the learning of a lesson, remembering to follow the pattern of the ages in praying, fasting and asking for a vision. So, then the lesson is shared once again by invoking the rituals of asking, praying and thanksgiving with the students. After learning the lesson and acknowledging the creation of knowledge, it is time to celebrate.

Celebration is the joyous acknowledgement of our ability to create and to be in the present as physical and spiritual beings, spreading light and exalting in the transformative process or "igniting the sparkle" (Cajete, 1972, p.237) for the student to hunt for knowledge to help the people. The story of *Beaver Teachings* is a light-hearted look at *Shinkyap*/Coyote *Spilahem* stories.

I believe we can live a satisfying multi-cultural life today. The completely egalitarian and inclusive nature *of Nlakapmux* philosophies recognize the intrinsic worth and value of all. The wholistic nature of our Indigenous world demands the involvement of everyone to become involved in educational processes in the home, community, or school. The connection to our future must be made from the present and the past. Grandmothers can resume their rightful place through the reconstruction and transmission of Indigenous knowledge to redefine learning place and space in our Indigenous families and communities, doing so proudly in the *Nlakapmux* way; thereby completing the circle/cycle of living a good life.

References

Allen, P. (1986). T*he sacred hoop, recovering the feminine in American Indian traditions*. Boston : Beacon Press

Archibald, J. (1992). Editorial: Giving voice to our ancestors. *Canadian Journal of Native Education 19(2)*, 141-44.

Archibald, J. (1997). *Coyote learns to make a story basket: The place of First Nations stories in education* (Unpublished doctoral dissertation). Simon Fraser University, Burnaby, British Columbia.

Archibald, J. (2008). *An Indigenous storywork methodology*. In J. Gary Knowles & Ardra Cole (Eds.), *Handbook of the arts in qualitative research: Perspectives, methodologies, examples, and issues* (pp. 371-384). Los Angeles: Sage Publications.

Archibald, J. (2008). *Indigenous storywork: Educating the heart, mind, body and spirit*. Vancouver: UBC Press.

Armstrong, J. (Ed.). (1993). *Looking at the words of our people: First Nations analysis of literature.* Penticton: Theytus Books.

Backhouse, F. (2010). The people's anthropologist. *British Columbia Magazine*, 52(3), 59-65.

Battiste, M. (Ed.) (2000). *Reclaiming Indigenous voice and vision.* Vancouver: UBC Press.

Battiste, M., & Henderson, J.Y. (1991). What is Indigenous knowledge? Approaches to Aboriginal knowledge, language and education. *Canadian Journal of Native Education, 22(*1), 16 – 27.

Battiste, M., & Henderson, J. Y. (2000). *Protecting Indigenous knowledge and heritage: A global challenge.* Saskatoon: Purich Press.

Boas, F. (1940). *Race, language, and culture*. New York: MacMillan Press.

Bouchard, R., & Kennedy, D. (1977). *Lillooet stories*. Victoria: Provincial Archives of British Columbia,

Bopp, J., Bopp, M., Brown, L., & Lane, P. (1982). *The sacred tree: Reflections on Native American spirituality*. Lethbridge: Four Worlds Development Press.

Brown, F. L. (2004). *Making the classroom a healthy place: The development of affective competency in Aboriginal pedagogy* (Unpublished doctoral dissertation). University of British Columbia, Vancouver, British Columbia.

Cajete, G. (1999). *A people's ecology: Explorations in sustainable living.* Santa Fe: Clear Light Publishing.

Cajete, G. (1994). *Look to the mountain: An ecology of Indigenous education.* New Mexico: Kivaki Press.

Calliou, S. (1996). *Shaking rattles in all directions: A case study/story of a female "Indian" student attending a Euro-Canadian university (1991-), located on the traditional territory of the Musqueam* (Unpublished doctoral dissertation). University of British Columbia, Vancouver, British Columbia.

Statistics Canada. (2008). *Aboriginal peoples in Canada in 2006: Inuit, Metis and First Nations, 2006 Census. Retrieved from http://www.statcan.gc.ca/daily-quotidien/080115/dq080115a-eng.htm.*

Castellano, M. B. (2000). Updating Aboriginal traditions of knowledge. In George Sefa Dei, Bud Hall & Dorothy Rosenberg, (Eds.), *Indigenous knowledges in global contexts: Multiple readings of our world* (pp. 21-36). Toronto: University of Toronto Press.

Chrisjohn, R., Young, S., & Maraun, M. (1997). *The circle game: Shadows and substance in the Indian Residential School experience in Canada.* Penticton: Theytus Books.

Cohen, B. (2001). The spider's web: Creativity to diversity in dynamic balance. *Canadian Journal of Native Education, 25*(2), 140 – 148.

Cohen, B. (2009). *School failed Coyote so fox built a new school* (Unpublished doctoral dissertation). University of British Columbia, Vancouver, British Columbia.

Crazybull, C. (2005). *Standing in the light: Culture as the heart of education.* SoTL Conference-CAU, January 17, 2005.

Cruikshank, J. (1990). *Life lived like a story, life stories of three Yukon Native Elders.* Vancouver: University of British Columbia Press.

Diaute, C., & Lightfoot, C. (Eds.) (2004). *Narrative analysis, studying the development of individuals in society.* New York: Sage Publications.

Du Bois, B. W. E. (1903). *The souls of black folk: Essays and sketches.* Chicago ILL: AC. McClurg & Co.

Freire, P. (1997). *Pedagogy of the oppressed.* New Revision 20th Anniversary Ed. New York: Continuum Press.

Freire, P. (2004). *Pedagogy of hope, reliving pedagogy of the oppressed* with notes *by Ana Maria Araujo Freire.* New York: Continuum Press.

Gardner, E. B. (2000). Where there are always wild strawberries. *Canadian Journal of Native Education, 24*(1), 7-13.

Grande, S. (2004). *Red pedagogy: Native American social and political thought.* New York, NY: Rowman & Littlefield Publishers Inc.

Graveline, J. F. (1998). *Circle works: Transforming Eurocentric consciousness.* Halifax: Fernwood Publishing.

Haeberlin, H. K., Teit, J. A., & Roberts, H. H. (1930). Coiled basketry in British Columbia and surrounding region. *American Anthropologist, New Series, 32*(2), 306 – 308.

Hanna, D., & Henry, M. (1995). *Our tellings: Interior Salish stories of the Nlha7kapmx people.* Vancouver: UBC Press.

Holmes, L. (2000). Heart knowledge, blood memory and the voice of the land: Implications of research among Hawaiian Elders. In George Sefa Dei, Bud Hall and Dorothy Rosenberg, (Eds.), *Indigenous knowledges in global contexts: Multiple readings of our world* (pp.37-53) Toronto: University of Toronto Press.

Howard-Bobiwash, H., Cole, S. C., & Bridgman, R. (1999). *Feminist fields: Ethnographic insights.* Toronto: University of Toronto Press.

Indian Act. (1952). Ottawa: Queens Printer.

Ing, R. (1991). The effects of Residential School on Native child-rearing practices. *Canadian Journal of Native Education, 18* (Supplement), 67 – 116.

Iseke, J. (2010). Importance of Metis ways of knowing in healing communities. *Canadian Journal of Native Education 33*(1), 83-97.

Kovach. M. (2009). *Indigenous methodologies: Characteristics, conversations, and contexts.* Toronto: University of Toronto Press.

Laforet, A., & York, A. (1999). *Spuzzum: Fraser Canyon histories, 1808 – 1939.* Vancouver: UBC Press.

Lane, P., Bopp, M., Bopp, J., & Brown, L. (1984). Elders' Teachings. Lethbridge: Four Worlds Development Press.

Marker, M. (2006). After the Maakah whalehunt : Indigenous Knowledge and limits to multicultural discourse. *Urban Education, 41*(5), 482-515.

Marseden, D. (2004). *Expanding knowledge through dreaming: Wampum and visual arts. Mississaugas of Scugog First Nation*. Vancouver BC: University of British Columbia. Retrieved September 18,2011 from http://www.pimatisiwin.com/uploads/1193385529.pdf.

McLeod, Y. (2003). Changemakers: Empowering Ourselves. *Canadian Journal of Native Education (27)*2, 108-126.

Miller, K.R. (1943). *Shingwauk's Vision: A history of Native Residential Schools,* Toronto: University of Toronto Press.
Ried, M., & Sewid-Smith, D. (2004). *Paddling to where I stand. Agnes Alfred, Qwiqwasutinuxw noblewoman.* Vancouver: University British Columbia Press.

Rigney, L. I. (1999). *Report – Inquiry into the effectiveness of education and training*. Adelaide: Hansard.

Rigney, L. I. (2003). *Indigenous education: The crisis of survival of Indigenous languages*. Monash, Faculty of Education Seminar Series, Wednesday, August 20, 1 – 2 pm, Clayton Campus.

Ross, R. (2006). *Returning to the teachings*. Canada: Penguin Books.

Sam, L. (2001). *Nak'azdli' t'enne Yahulduk/Nak'azdli Elders speak.* Penticton: Theytus Book Ltd.

Silko, L. (2006). *Ceremony*. Worldwide: Penguin Books.

Smith, G. H. (1997). *The development of Kaupapa Maori: Theory and Praxis* (Unpublished doctoral dissertation) University of Auckland, New Zealand.

Smith, L. T. (1999). *Decolonizing methodologies: Research and Indigenous peoples*. New York: Zed Books Ltd.

Smith, G. H. (2000). Protecting and respecting Indigenous Knowledge. In Marie Battiste, (Ed.), *Reclaiming Indigenous voice and vision* (pp. 209-224). Vancouver: UBC Press.

Smith, L. T. (2000). Kaupapa Maori Research. In Marie Battiste (Ed.) *Reclaiming Indigenous voice and vision, (*pp. 225-247). Vancouver: UBC Press

Smith, G. H. (2003). *Indigenous struggle for the transformation of education of schooling*. Keynote Address to the Alaskan Federation of Natives (AFN) Convention. Anchorage, Alaska.

Sterling, S. (1992). *My name is Seepeetza*. Toronto: Groundwood Douglas Books.

Sterling, S. (1997). *The Grandmother stories* (Unpublished doctoral Dissertation). University of British Columbia, Vancouver, British Columbia.

Sterling, L. S. (2002). *Breaking illusions and transforming voice: Indigenous culture and its role in multigenerational trauma and healing* (Unpublished doctoral dissertation) University of British Columbia, Vancouver, British Columbia.

Stigter, S. (2003). *Double-voice and double-consciousness in Native American literature*. Lethbridge: University of Lethbridge.

Stigter, S. (2008). *Two worldviews: Double-voice and double-consciousness.* New York: Amazon Books.

Teit, J. A. (1898). *Traditions of the Thompson Indians of British Columbia. Collected and Annotated by James Teit.* Ottawa: Canadian Museum of Civilization.

Teit, J. A. (1900). *The Thompson Indians*. *Memoir # 2.* American Museum of Natural History, New York: American Museum of Natural History.

Teit, J. A., Haeberlin, Karl H., & Roberts, Helen H. (1900). *The Thompson Indians of British Columbia*. New York: American Museum of Natural History.

Teit, J. A. (1912). *The mythology of the Thompson Indians*. New York: American Museum of Natural History.

Teit, J. A., Haeberlin, Karl H., Roberts, Helen H., & Boas, Franz. (1928). *Coiled basketry in British Columbia and surrounding regions*. Washington: Smithsonian Institution.

Teit, J. A. (1912). *Traditions of the Lillooet Indians of British Columbia. Washington*: Smithsonian Museum.

Teit, J. A. (1916). *The European tales of the Upper Thompson Indians. Washington*: Smithsonian Museum.

Teit, J. A. (1917). *Folktales of Salishan and Sahaptin Indians of British Columbia. Washington*: Smithsonian Museum.

Teit, J. A. (1930). *The Salish Tribes of the Western Plateau of British Columbia. Washington*: Smithsonian Museum.

Tepper, L. H. (1987). *The Interior Salish Tribes of British Columbia: A photographic collection*. Hull, QUE: National Museums of Canada.

Thompson, L., & Thompson, T. (1996). *Thompson River dictionary*. ISBN#879763-12-5; UMOPL No. 12.

Van Eijk, J. P. (2010). *Traditional First Nations languages boundless*. University of Regina Report. June 14, 2010.

Vedan, R. (2002). *How do we forgive our fathers: Angry/Violent Aboriginal/First Nations men's experiences with social workers* (Unpublished doctoral dissertation). Simon Fraser University, Burnaby, British Columbia.

White, E., & Archibald, J. (1999). Kwulasulwut s yuth: Ellen White's Teachings. *Canadian Journal of Native Education, 19*(2), 150-164.

Wickwire, W., & McGonigle, M. (1988). *Stein, the way of the river*. Vancouver: Talon Books.

Wickwire, W. (1988). James A. Teit: His contribution to Canadian ethnomusicology. *Journal of Native Studies, 8*(2), 183 – 204.

Wickwire, W. (1998). We shall drink from the stream and so shall you: James A. Teit and Native resistance in British Columbia, 1908 – 1922. *Canadian Historical Review, 79*(2) 199 – 237.

York, A. (1990). *Thompson ethnobotany: Knowledge and usage of plants by the Thompson Indians of British Columbia.* Victoria: Royal British Columbia Museum.

York, A., Daly, R., & Arnett, C. (1993). *They write their dreams on the rocks forever: Rock writings in the Stein River Valley of British Columbia*. Boston: Allyn & Bacon Press.

Young-Ing, G. (2006). *Intellectual property rights, legislated protection, sui generis models and ethical access in the transformation of Indigenous traditional knowledge* (Unpublished doctoral dissertation). University of British Columbia, Vancouver, British Columbia.

Appendix A: Questions for the Nlakapmux Grandmothers

1. What is your earliest memory of your maternal/paternal Grandmother?

2. Can you recall a time that she taught you something, that today we would call cultural knowledge? Please share that remembrance with me.

3. What is your favourite story about how your Grandmother passed on her teachings to you?

4. What cultural teaching(s) do you remember? How did she teach you?

5. How old were you then?

6. What *Nlakapmux* learning activities did you share with her in these life phases?

   a. As a child?
   b. As a youth (through your teens)?
   c. As a young adult?

d. After you had children?

7. Were there some ways that she taught you that were similar throughout your life phases? I so, what were they? Why are these teaching/learning approaches so memorable? Were there challenges or difficulties that you experienced learning from her?

8. Have you used any of these ways of teaching/learning with your own children? If yes, please share them and tell me why you continue to use them. If not, can you tell me why not?

9. If you use these ways of teaching, have they changed from how she used them? If yes, please tell me how. If no, please tell how you are able to keep these traditional ways of teaching current in today's changing world.
   a. What memory of your Grandmother is sacred to you? Why?

10. Name three teachings she imparted to you.

11. Why are these important enough that you have named them?

12. Do you use them in your family and personal life?

13. How can *Nlakapmux* oral tradition and traditional teachings about living a good life, contribute to learning among *Nlakapmux* families?

Printed by
Schaltungsdienst Lange o.H.G., Berlin